The Hogarth Plays

Nick Dear's plays include *Dedication* (Nuffield Theatre, Southampton, 2016.), *The Dark Earth and the Light Sky* (Almeida Theatre, 2012), *Frankenstein* (National Theatre, 2011), *Lunch in Venice* (National Theatre Connections, 2005), *Power* (NT, 2003), *The Villains' Opera* (NT, 2000), *Zenobia* (RSC, 1995), *In the Ruins* (Bristol Old Vic, 1990), *Food of Love* (Theatre de Complicite, Almeida, 1988), *The Art of Success* (RSC, 1986), *Pure Science* (RSC, 1986) and *Temptation* (RSC, 1984). He also collaborated with Peter Brook on the development of *Qui est là?* (Bouffes du Nord, 1996). His adaptations include *The Promise* (after Arbuzov, Tricycle, 2002), *Summerfolk* (after Gorky, NT, 1999), *Le Bourgeois Gentilhomme* (after Molière, NT, 1992), *The Last Days of Don Juan* (after Tirso de Molina, RSC, 1990) and *A Family Affair* (after Ostrovsky, Cheek by Jowl, 1988). His screenplays include *Persuasion*, *The Turn of the Screw*, *Cinderella*, *The Gambler*, *Byron*, *Eroica* and *Agatha Christie's Poirot*. Opera libretti include *The Palace in the Sky* (ENO/Hackney Empire, 2001) and *Siren Song* (Almeida Opera Festival, 1994). He has also written extensively for BBC Radio, beginning with his first play, *Matter Permitted* (1980).

T0322882

NICK DEAR

The Hogarth Plays

THE ART OF SUCCESS
THE TASTE OF THE TOWN

FABER & FABER

This two-play edition first published in 2018
by Faber and Faber Ltd
The Bindery, 51 Hatton Garden,
London EC1N 8HN

Typeset by Country Setting, Kingsdown, Kent CT14 8ES
Printed and bound by CPI Group (UK) Ltd, Croydon CR0 4YY

A CIP record for this book
is available from the British Library

ISBN 978-0-571-35016-2

4 6 8 10 9 7 5

For Penny

who has been with me for both of these plays
and the thirty years in between

Introduction

Revisiting your younger self is a peculiar experiment, and not one that should be attempted at home.

When I decided to write a sequel to *The Art of Success*, some thirty years after I'd written the original, I didn't think it would be too difficult to slip back into the voice of the earlier play. Of course, I was wrong.

I sat down to re-inhabit the skin of the person I used to be, and found that much had changed, more so than I was expecting. Not only had my views on what might constitute a good play undergone a revision, or two or three, but also what I thought I wanted from art, from life, from the whole damn thing, was subtly different. I was the same person as before – obviously – yet somehow not quite the same. So you start to ask, well, who is actually 'me', then?

The 'me' who wrote the early play was angry about everything, which was fortunate, as my main character was angry about everything, too. One of the ways in which my life has changed since then is that I became a father. Now my sons are adults, and perhaps looking back on their younger selves; it's hard to be angry about everything when your life is enriched by children.

In other ways, also, my outlook is different. The first play is set in the city, the second in the country. The first play takes place mainly at night, the second during the day. Both purport to be about art, but are really about anything but art. The voice is the same – it has to be –

yet the idiolect appears to have altered. How? I think only someone who isn't 'me' will be able to tell!

My two leading characters in *The Taste of the Town* are, like their author, thirty years older. Whether any of us is wiser is debatable. But it was fun spending time with them again, and I hope they felt the same about me.

Nick Dear
September 2018

THE ART OF SUCCESS

The Art of Success was first performed by the Royal Shakespeare Company at The Other Place, Stratford upon Avon, on 2 July 1986. The play transferred to the Pit Theatre at the Barbican on 13 August 1987. The cast was as follows:

Jane Hogarth Niamh Cusack
William Hogarth Michael Kitchen
Henry Fielding Philip Franks
Frank David Killick
Oliver Simon Russell Beale
Mrs Needham Dilys Laye
Louisa Dinah Stabb
Sarah Sprackling Penny Downie
Robert Walpole Joe Melia
Queen Caroline Susan Porrett

Other parts were played by members of the company.

Director Adrian Noble
Designer Ultz
Music Paul Reade

The Art of Success was later performed in repertoire with *The Taste of the Town* at Rose Theatre Kingston on 13 September 2018. The cast, in alphabetical order, was as follows:

Jane Hogarth Ruby Bentall
Louisa Emma Cunniffe
Frank Ben Deery
Henry Fielding Jack Derges
William Hogarth Bryan Dick
Oliver Ian Hallard
Queen Caroline Susannah Harker
Sarah Sprackling Jasmine Jones
Mrs Needham Sylvestra Le Touzel
Robert Walpole Mark Umbers

Director Anthony Banks
Set and Costume Designer Andrew D. Edwards
Video and Projection Designer Douglas O'Connell
Lighting Designer James Whiteside
Music Olly Fox
Sound Designer Max Pappenheim
Casting Director Stuart Burt
Fight Directors Rachel Bown Williams and
    Ruth Cooper Brown of RC-Annie Ltd
Movement Naomi Said
Assistant Director Ally Manson

Characters

Jane Hogarth
William Hogarth
Harry Fielding
Frank
Oliver
Mrs Needham
Louisa
Sarah Sprackling
Robert Walpole
Queen Caroline

Act One

London in the 1730s. The Beefsteak Club. A group of drunken men asleep at a table in the middle of the afternoon. They have collapsed amongst the debris of a huge meal. They snore contentedly.

A woman (Jane) enters stealthily. She circles the men in quiet anger. She makes out the one she's looking for (William). She raises a large pair of scissors, then puts them between William's legs. There is a loud 'snip' and William wakes in panic. Jane exits. He doesn't see her.

William No! Jane! Don't!

He jumps away from the table and examines himself, but nothing has happened to him.

Christ, what a bitch.

Harry *(waking)* What is it, Will?

William My wife, she –

William looks under the table for her. She's not there.

Nothing. A dream. My head is full of nightmares.

Harry It's the rich food and drink.

William It's the cuts of beef, the blood-red beef –

Harry The cheddar –

William The quantity of ale. The dreams get worse the more you gorge. It's as if the brain, it fractures open, and horrible creatures spew hot from its crack.

Harry I thought you said it was your wife.

William Well, yes, it was Janey, but she was – she had her dressmaking shears and she – well, let's just say it's not what I had hoped for from a marriage.

Harry You regret it already?

William Don't talk daft.

Frank (*stirs and mumbles*) Minutes of the Annual General Meeting of . . .

Harry Tell me your dreams, if they're upsetting you.

William They're not upsetting me, nothing's upsetting me, there's just some bastard forever chipping away in my bloody sleep, carving away at my sense of myself, and why? Why? Is it envy of my talent or what is it?

Harry It's all this boozing at lunchtime.

William I know, I know, and the pressure of work.

Harry And you have a lively imagination and you –

William Lively? It's running fucking riot, mate!

Frank (*stands, uncertainly, pissed*) Minutes of the Annual General Meeting of the Sublime Society of Beefsteaks, held in Mrs Needham's upstairs room this afternoon the –

Harry Meeting's adjourned, Frank.

Frank Normal agenda. Election of officers.

William Shut up, Frank.

Frank Officers re-elected without contest, as per last year. Minutes read and agreed with no dissent. Treasurer's report revealed a surplus in the bank and as per usual all new applications for membership of our estimable Club were unanimously rejected. Whereupon the Secretary volunteered the observation that the Society of Beefsteaks could well be said to mirror in little the happy torpor of our kingdom as a whole.

Harry Tell that to the poor of Dorset.

William Shut up, Harry.

Frank The membership thereupon with due and proper ceremony devoured the half-cooked rump of a bullock, sang several rather long songs of dubious tastefulness, burped a bit, farted a bit, and drank themselves into oblivion. (*Sits.*)

William A vote of thanks, to the Secretary.

Oliver (*his head on the table*) Seconded.

Frank (*rises*) Gratefully accepted. (*Sits.*)

William What about a small drink?

Frank (*rises*) We now proceed to Any Other Business, William.

Harry What's that, Frank?

William Oh no. Not me.

Oliver Hark at the newlywed.

William I don't want to catch nothing, do I.

Frank Wear your armour.

William I've chucked it away.

Frank They'll wash one out for you, I'm sure, they always have some spares.

Harry Spare what? What are you talking about?

Oliver The dried gut of a sheep.

Frank Cundums, boy. Are you telling us you've never worn one?

Harry No . . .

Frank Are you telling us you've never – had it off?

Harry No! But I've never been with a rented woman. Always gone with nice girls. When mother's back is turned. You don't fiddle about with a length of intestine in front of a girl from a genteel house. You discharge your obligations at once.

William Very gratifying.

Frank Dangerous, though.

William Not with your wife.

Frank Not with yours, perhaps. But my beloved . . . the sight of her unlaced would turn your thing to mush. (*Imploring.*) William . . .!

William No, I've got work to do before the daylight goes. And I said I'd meet Jane for a walk.

Frank A walk! The change in the man! Where once the fires of lust roared in his gut, now all is calm and sensible, a candle-flame of passion.

Harry I burn, though, Frank. I smoulder.

Frank You?

Harry Yes, I'm in the market. I believe a writer should sample every experience.

Frank Then I move: that this Annual General Meeting invite our good friend Mrs Needham to offer us a selection of her stock, the Meeting having a view to purchase, and the necessary funds being made available by the Society.

Oliver Seconded.

William It's not coming out of the kitty?

Harry Don't see why not. Treasurer's just seconded it.

William (*outraged*) Fuck off!

Frank William, this is a formally-constituted AGM, please speak through the chair if you have a point of order.

William Are you trying to tell me that you lot intend getting your collective leg over and paying for it out of my bleeding subs?

Oliver Yes, we are. Absolutely, yes.

William Are you fuck! That's never fair!

Oliver Yes it is.

William What, you mean I lose out just because I love my wife?

Harry Will –

William What, mate?

Harry You always drink more than your share. (*Laughter.*)

William (*beaten*) You tight-fisted shits . . .

Oliver Oh, stop complaining. Potter off home to the warmth of the bridal couch.

William He desired my wife himself, you know. He would come sniffing round her doorway like an over-eager pup. When I was already inside.

Oliver This kennel-talk is witty.

William Is it. Then why don't you sod off and play with your bone?

Oliver I'm only concerned for a fellow-member's welfare.

William He's jealous!

Oliver What is it, don't she come on heat quite as frequent as one might prefer? Or is it – dear Janey's a lovely tall bint, isn't she? – is it just too high for the mongrel to reach? I mean I've heard of marrying above oneself but this is –

Frank Oliver –

Oliver – fucking ridiculous.

William (*makes a run at Oliver*) Come here, I'll cripple you!

William is restrained by Frank and Harry.

Oliver Oh, the upstart's frightfully drunk.

William Of course I'm drunk, what do you think I come here for, the company?

Oliver I am a peer of the realm – I could ruin your career!

William I'll pull your purple bollocks off, that'll fuck your pedigree!

Frank Gentlemen, please, behave like Beefsteaks! – Will, apologise to the Viscount.

Harry And Oliver, shake hands with a great artist.

Oliver A great artist? The runt with the inky fingers? A great artist? We talk a different language, Mr Fielding. Willy Hogarth, a great artist? Let us assess his curriculum vitae. What cathedrals has he done? What frescos of what battles? What mansion walls adorned with Roman heroes? What royal features stippled with immortal pigment?

William My portraits are widely reputed to be –

Oliver Oh, portraits, portraits, any hack can do titchy portraits to clutter up sideboards, but a great artist – Let me remind you one has toured the Continent and one has *seen* great art, I mean the originals, vast canvases in gold leaf frames, huge blocks of stone chipped up to holiness, Annunciation, Pietà, and in the damp palaces of Venice spent my inheritance, spent money like water building my collection of Madonnas –

William Dead Christs, Holy Families, flying fucking angels, and ship-loads no doubt of similar dismal, dark subjects.

Oliver Historical allegories, mainly, drawn from the well of antique myth.

William Which no one can understand.

Oliver Not open to the common herd, I grant you.

William Which *I* can't understand.

Oliver Lack of education is such a dreary thing.

William I didn't have time for an education, I had to earn a crust. I have no patron, no office, no inheritance, but what I do have is this body of work behind me, built from nothing. It's not great, not quite, but not inconsiderable, though I've flogged some shit I know, some rotten illustrations, but I do believe, I must allow myself to believe I have it in me – great work! Lasting work! I mean I am still learning, yes, I'm not exactly a prodigy, Christ, I hate prodigies, I've hated prodigies since I was about twenty-five years old, but fucking hell I'm making a fucking go of it, aren't I? (*He goes and sits in a corner and sulks.*)

Oliver . . . Something I said?

Harry You ought to see his latest work, it's bloody good.

Oliver Oh? What is the subject?

Harry A harlot.

Oliver A harlot? What, a tart? Oh, jolly well done, Will, a picture of a tart –

William Six pictures.

Oliver Six?

Harry He calls it a Progress.

Oliver Six pictures of a whore? Progress? That is utterly silly. What chap of any character or standing is going to want to be seen buying six pictures of a prostitute, for heaven's sake?

Harry Well, I've ordered a set of prints.

Frank Me too, the wife wants some.

Oliver Oh, prints, well, prints, absolutely, naturally one shall have a set of prints oneself, but one is talking about paintings, canvases, one is talking about art. Art rests in the original, not the copy.

Harry Does it?

Oliver Why certainly. Anyone can own a copy. Genius is not shared around like a bag of peppermints.

Frank Buy the originals, then. You've got the cash.

William They're not for sale. Not to him, who covets my wife.

Oliver See? He's petrified.

William (*returning*) Of what am I petrified?

Oliver That your work will not stand compare with the fruits of my Grand Tour. How can a man who has barely been south of the Thames seriously aspire to be a painter?

William What is art?

Oliver Now let's not split hairs.

William No, what is art – property? Or communication? Does it exist to be owned, or to be understood?

Oliver I think I'll just nip downstairs and have a word with Mrs Needham.

William Do you know what I'm talking about?

Oliver No, damn you, but I know what I like.

William And what do you like?

Oliver Well . . . As a rule, William . . . Something with a certain 'je ne sais quoi', that's what I usually go for.

Exit Oliver with a superior air.

Frank That is the great benefit of a Club such as ours. The interchange of ideas between men of civilisation and intelligence – A picture's a picture, I would have said.

William But what if every bloke in the street can own a masterpiece for sixpence? Then where are your connoisseurs? Your gentlemen collectors?

Frank I never imagined you as a champion of the heaving masses.

William Champion my arse. I want their sixpences. I reckon I can as well get a living by dealing with the public in general, as by hanging on the whims and fancies of the rich. In fact I could be very wealthy.

Frank Then why aren't you?

William Because of the pirates. The bastard pirates of print. Some geezer will come round my place posing as a buyer for the original painting, and the next thing you know there'll be a shoddy bloody copy of it in the shops before I've even got the acid off my etching, and then they'll knock down my payments because the market's flooded with imitations – it makes you weep!

Frank But surely you have copyright on your design?

Harry No, he doesn't, because it's very hard to legislate for the ownership of an idea. The thunder and lightning in your head. Writers were only granted protection of our ideas a few years ago. There's nothing that covers the specific problems of engravers.

Frank I'm only a simple merchant. The world of art is strange to me, all I know anything about is life. Now, in life, if I've a boat-load of sugar, say, or blacks, or molasses, I expect to have a document to prove I own the cargo, and I don't expect a soul to challenge it, or if they do that's stealing and they'll hang. We have greatly widened the scope of the capital offence under Mr Walpole. Can you identify your pirates?

William 'Course I can, they're all old mates.

Frank Then you must have redress.

William What, you mean like, take them round the back of the printshop and –

Frank No, man, in the courts! Go through the courts! Use the law, it's made for you. Whether you like it or not, you're a businessman now.

William (*thoughtful*) Art as business. Yes.

Harry But you'd have to get the law changed, Frank. You'd have to get a Bill through parliament.

Frank Then petition parliament. That's what it's for. It's made up of perfectly ordinary fellows, Harry, very like me if the truth be known, and very understanding of another fellow's needs.

Harry You mean it's a corrupt little clique whose sole reason for existence is to line its own pockets.

William Run by Robert Walpole . . .

Harry Precisely, that's why I ridicule him in every play I've ever written. In the new one I represent him as a –

Frank Don't tell me, don't spoil it, I'm coming to the show! Oliver and I are going to drum up some trade for you.

Harry What, tonight? Thanks very much.

Frank (*to William*) No doubt you've satirised the Great Man as well, have you? It being so much the fashion.

William No, not him personally, I haven't.

Harry Then now's your chance, Will! What a chance! 'The Harlot's Progress' is going to be a huge success. Why don't you follow it up with a political one? Why don't you do a 'Statesman's Progress' and drag our tyrant through the mud?

William No.

Harry Why not? Depicting how he bribed his way to power?

William No.

Harry It'll sell in tens of thousands!

William There are more important things in life than money, Henry!

Harry Yes, I'm talking about them!

William I said no, didn't I?

Harry But you never said why not.

William Look, I know you're my best mate and all –

Harry Well, I used to be.

William But if there's one thing I won't do it's peddle second-hand ideas, Harry, because I'm not interested in theories, I'm interested in people – you get bogged down in theory, you never reach into yourself –

Harry We're above it, are we? We're untouched by the world?

William Nobody tells me what to paint! – I'm bursting for a slash. (*Exits.*)

Frank Ah, the tactical widdle, veteran of many a boardroom skirmish.

Harry (*bitter*) Interested in people . . .! I remember a time when no one was safe from the blade of his graving-tool. The rich and the mighty and the idiotic chiselled out in black and white. Simple monochrome of judgement.

Frank Attack, attack, attack, it's all attack with you. Some things are worth defending – stable government for one. Learn a little balance, or the Prime Minister will close you down.

Harry He can't, I'm far too popular.

William (*returning*) The bucket's gone – what shall I do?

Frank Into the street. I think I'll join you.

Harry Now you come to mention it –

All three piss out of the window with sighs of relief.

Frank Bet you a tanner you can't get it in that window.

Pause.

William You owe me a tanner.

They giggle. Unseen by them, Mrs Needham enters with Oliver. She peers at the men.

Mrs Needham You'll get another drop out of that if you wring it.

Frank Mrs Needham!

The pissers are embarrassed.

Mrs Needham We, too, live in the sight of God, remember. This is a respectable street! How would you like it if I came and urinated over your neighbours?

They all approve of the idea.

Cheeky devils. What is it you want, then? Don't be bashful, we must have a proper order. The goods are stored below, it only remains to make a requisition. (*She takes out a notebook and checks off a list.*) May God forgive me what I do. My constant prayer is that I might make enough from this commerce to leave off in good time to atone. You, young man, what sort of a slut is your heart's desire?

Harry gawps.

They're all quite clean and they go to church on Sundays. I've got Peggy free, she's a little fat one, she will rub you in her bosom till you come off in her face, she doesn't mind, she's used to it, what do you say to that?

Harry Er, I –

Mrs Needham Good, that's you sorted.

Frank Elizabeth – don't make it difficult for us.

Mrs Needham It's not me making it difficult, Frank, it's the Lord. And I hope you've lost your taste for stinging nettles. I had a rash for a week.

Frank You weren't holding them right. If you hold them right you don't get stung.

Mrs Needham That's if you hold them with your hands, Frank. Now then, you sir – what can I tempt you with? Birch twigs? Leather face-mask? Would you care to join a filthy masquerade?

William No, I don't think I would, thank you.

Mrs Needham Boys, is it? I've got boys if you want them.

William No, it isn't boys! It's – I – it's because I – oh, fuck.

The others laugh at him. Stumped for an explanation, he turns and leaves angrily.

Mrs Needham Some people shock very easy. But not my favourite Viscount. I have a treat for a regular customer. I have a little virgin, a real one mind, nothing sewn up or otherwise embroidered, an innocent young beauty I've been schooling in the sciences of lust, and for an extra guinea you may shag her infant brains out, if you wish . . .

Pause. Oliver takes out his purse and drops it on the table. Blackout.

SCENE TWO

A pleasure garden. Amongst the classical statuary and symmetrical borders stands Louisa, on the lookout for trade.

Louisa (*shivers*) Wind off the Thames blows down the avenues, round the rotunda, through the triumphal arches and directly up my skirt. I must have the coldest

legs in England. A sailor in a Bermondsey cellar said that
in China they tell of a wind disease, a cold, cold wind
blowing round the body, typhoon in your arms and legs,
whispering draughts at the back of your skull. I told him
I think I've got it, mate, it all sounds dead familiar. He
laughed and bit my nipple with splintering teeth. What
I would have loved, at that moment, what I longed for,
was that all the air would whoosh out of me like a burst
balloon, and I sink down to nothing at his feet, and
teach the disbelieving rat a lesson. Here I am out in all
weathers, all the entrances and exits in my body open to
the elements day and freezing night, what's to stop the
gale when it comes in and fills me? And blows round my
bones for ever? – Wait, is he walking this way? That
dragoon? He looks so sad . . . doesn't he look sad . . .
I don't know, they call this place a pleasure garden, I've
never seen such misery, I'd christen it the garden of wind
and disappointment, or cold and frosted cunt.

Jane has entered, unseen. She listens.

Is he coming over here? Come along, then, miss, get all
your gusts and breezes together . . .
   Nice time with an old windbag, soldier? It's not
wearing any knickers.
   (*She promenades. She sees Jane.*) And what do you
want, may I ask?

Jane Aren't you cold? You look blue.

Louisa Well who's going to want to shaft a shiverer
wrapped from head to foot in rags? You have to show a
man a bit of skin.

Jane Why don't you wear some stockings, at least?

Louisa (*mimes being strangled*) That's why. And they
never see the goose-pimples. Lust is a great blinder, oh
isn't it just. – Oh farts, he's wandering off. That was you

23

done that. He must've thought we're only working doubles.

Jane I do beg your pardon. I couldn't help overhearing – I couldn't tear myself away. Please let me give you some money.

Louisa What have I got to do for it?

Jane Why, nothing. Take it. You have the most appalling life, don't you?

Louisa . . . Are you looking for an unusual experience?

Jane Um, I don't think so.

Louisa Because it makes me livid. Young ladies of quality coming down here, all for an hour of rough sex.

Jane Oh dear.

Louisa Taking the bread right out of our mouths!

Jane You have my sympathy.

Louisa Good. (*She hits Jane.*) Then perhaps you'll heed a gentle warning. Stay off my patch! You won't enjoy it. Soft skin bruise up like a peach. And what about the bite-marks and the blood?

Jane You misunderstand, I'm waiting for my –

Louisa hits her again.

Ow! – I suppose if you are forced to live like an animal you are going to start to behave like one.

Louisa Don't call me an animal. Animals don't do this for a living.

William enters.

William Janey, there you are.

Jane You're late. I've had to send the carriage away and I've had to wait here alone.

Louisa (*staring pointedly at William*) I don't know you from somewhere, do I, sir?

William (*rigid with panic*) I shouldn't think so, no.

Jane My husband is actually rather famous. It is possible you may have had him pointed out to you in town.

Louisa That must be it. I thought he looked familiar.

Jane He is an artist.

Louisa Well isn't that a nice thing to be? A profession as old as my own.

Jane William, this poor woman is a prostitute.

William Oh, is she?

Jane She is forced to solicit for custom even in this foul weather. Isn't that shaming? To you, I mean? A man? – What is your name?

Louisa Louisa, madam.

Jane Louisa, I hold nothing against you. But for the accident of birth I . . . Oh, the trade in flesh, isn't it pernicious.

William Yes, but there's nothing we can do about it today.

Jane Perhaps there is. Perhaps if we took this woman home and gave her a hot meal and a bath, she might regain her – self respect –

William You're joking!

Louisa (*shivers tragically*) The wind . . . The wind blows through the warmest men, and turns their hearts as cold as stone. There's a bloke over there by the Temple of Virtue, I think he's wanting business. Excuse me. (*Exits, flashing a leg at William.*)

Jane And where I wonder will she sleep tonight?

William Up Drury Lane by the Queen's Head, that's – oh – that's where they all live, Janey, isn't it? Up Drury Lane? Them back alleys?

Jane I brought your basket. With roast beef and beer – Will, you don't have anything to do with such women, do you? Not now we're together?

William No, never, never, I swear it. Temptation comes my way sometimes but I am strong and I resist it. Save myself for you. And your little cheeks red from the wind. (*Kisses her.*)

Jane Imagine them out here . . . brr! . . . having to . . .

William (*interested*) What?

Jane You know. Up against the trees, the rough bark in your hair, linen down in the leaf-mould . . .

William You find it – exciting?

Jane Not so much exciting as just –

William Dirty.

Jane A tightness at the back of the throat and I –

William Sordid.

Jane Well . . .

William But somewhere down in the dregs of your mind you –

Jane Yes – ?

William Jane, I love you, let's get on the floor.

Jane I beg your pardon!

William It's not very wet.

He tries to drag her down.

Jane William! Are you out of your mind!

William Yes, yes, I'm berserk for you, come on darling, you're my prize –

Jane This is a public place!

William – my reward for being good, give it to me Janey –

Jane I'm sorry but I can't!

William – open your lovely knees!

Jane breaks away. Pause.

Jane I thought we were going out for a walk . . .!

William Oh, fuck.

Jane What sort of woman . . . What sort of woman is it you want me to be? You seem to want to make me something I am not.

William I'm trying. I am trying! There aren't many men who understand women at all, you know.

Jane Understand women . . .?

William Yes, well, I'm making a bleeding effort, at least.

Jane An effort?

William Yes an effort! Do I force you? Do I ever? Hot with humiliation in the Vauxhall mud and do I complain? No, I try to understand.

Jane He thinks he understands. Hallelujah! Pass the paintpot! Pass the pedestal, let me get on! – God, the limitless arrogance of them.

William Thanks very much, Jane, that's just the gesture of support I was hoping for.

Jane I love you, I love you, idiot! But you take so much for granted! That I will need you when you need me. That I will be clean but dirty, ignorant but clever. That I will have a mind of my own that you can say you're proud of. Loving you is such a struggle . . . hand-to-hand every inch of the way . . . I am enmeshed in you, and I don't always like it. But it happens! It happens! I am a tangle of things not easily unravelled. So please, don't go round thinking you begin to understand me. Just love me. That's all. Just accept. Because I refuse to be understood.

William (*pause. He averts his eyes*) I'll see you tonight.

Exit William with basket. Jane takes a step after him, then stops with a gesture of anger and frustration. Fade to black.

SCENE THREE

A prison cell. Piles of dirt and straw. A high barred window and heavy door. A table and chair, and a stool. Sarah sits at the table, sunk in daydreams. There is a woman's cry, far away in the depths of the gaol. Sarah comes to, blinking. She pays no attention to the cry. She empties the contents of a jug of water into a bowl: about half a cupful. With a sigh of annoyance she rolls up her sleeves and prepares to wash herself. Then changes her mind, picks up the bowl and goes to drink. Then changes her mind again, puts it down, and washes her grimy arms and face. When finished she looks into the water with distaste. She arranges her filthy clothes as neatly as she can. She has a silver spoon concealed in a

*pocket. She polishes it up and checks her reflection.
She smells her breath, pokes at a rotting tooth. She puts
the spoon away and looks at the water again. Then in
one swift movement she grabs the bowl, drinks the
water, and sets it back on the table again as if it hadn't
happened. She stares ahead with an innocent look.
The bolts on the far side of the door are drawn back.
A Gaoler shows William into the cell. He carries his
basket. He sniffs the air and recoils.*

Sarah You came then. I weren't sure.

She extends her hand to him.

Gaoler Sir, the fever in a gaol . . . They say you feel it
dance beneath the skin . . . Like a fire in a turf-moor,
never put it out. If you're lucky you go mad before you
die.

William Cheers, I look forward to it. (*Shakes Sarah's
hand.*)

Gaoler I have to bolt the door, has this been explained?

William Yes, but do it quietly, I've got a miserable
headache and I'm not in a very good mood.

Gaoler You can still change your mind.

William I've been in a nick before. Grew up in the
shadow of the walls. Father a debtor, poor old bugger.
Done well for myself, though, haven't I? (*Shows off his
clothes.*)

Gaoler Yes, sir, you have.

William Obviously being terrorised at an impressionable
age by shits with whips and manacles provides a first-
rate training for the wider world.

Sarah laughs. The Gaoler turns nasty.

Gaoler I'm going to lock you in, now, sir, in the bowels of Newgate, all right?

The Gaoler leaves and locks the door.

Sarah It is an honour to meet you.

William The light in here is rubbish. Rubbish.

Sarah Your eyes soon get accustomed.

William But the smell – the excrement of fear – that takes me back.

Sarah I'm sorry about the pong but –

William Don't be.

Sarah – there's an open sewer –

William Dung does not disgust me. Quite the contrary. It reminds us what we are. I refuse to let myself be offended by any human functions.

Sarah Very nice it must be, having the choice.

William I see you have a flicker of wit. How would you like to be – preserved?

Sarah Don't care.

William 'Course you do.

Sarah No I don't.

William Are you going to mess me about?

Sarah I don't care!

William But your appearance – you've gone to some trouble – I'm amazed you can keep as clean as that in this fuck-awful place. The power of a woman's self-respect! – Or am I being condescending, sorry if I am.

Sarah I ain't gone to any bother.

William Sit you at the table I think.

She sits.

Background of barred window and bolted door. I'd like to do something with the stench. The way the air hangs heavy with disease, drip of plague like dew . . . But how do you show a smell, I wonder? How do you paint an aroma?

Sarah You can't, it's impossible.

William Not if you have any art. You might for example draw someone holding a scented handkerchief to their nose, standing nearby and, what could they be – glancing at the pisspot?

Sarah How do we know it is scented?

William What?

Sarah This hankie. This feller, he could be just blowing.

William Perfume bottle –

Sarah Oh, good.

William – peeping from the pocket of his coat.

William sits on the stool and prepares his sketching board.

Sarah You got a bit of a brain, too, haven't you?

William Ta, yes, as a nipper I was apprenticed to a silver engraver, my widowed mum being very poor, and since then I've developed this system of like visual language, this technical memory, which is unique in that it –

Sarah How do I know it is perfume?

William What?

Sarah In the bottle.

William Well of course it's perfume.

Sarah Could be water.

William Well it's not.

Sarah Could be gin.

William It's perfume!

Sarah But how do I know?

William Because it's written on the side! 'Perfume'!

Sarah No it's not.

William It is, it is!

Sarah (*bangs table*) Look, prick, it's bloody well not.

William (*wary of her*) . . . Why not?

Sarah 'Cause I can't bloody well read, that's why not. Is it so much, that I should understand?

Pause. William begins to work.

William Sketching in chalk and pencil, Sarah. Won't take long. Sorry I was late, been rushing round town all day, I'm so bloody busy it's not real. On my way here I thought I would put in the Gaoler. With his keys and whip. But that would kind of prejudge the case, wouldn't it?

Sarah Good, I can live without him breathing down me neck.

William Does he pester you? I could have a word with the Governor or someone.

Sarah He daren't come near me. He's scared I cut his throat. (*Laughs.*) Would too. That brute. I seen him rub his self. He'll prob'ly wait till I'm done for, then he'll stick it in. Then he'll turn me over to the surgeons.

William Haven't you got no family to –

Sarah What, hang on me legs? They say it's a blessing if you can get someone to hang on your legs, don't they? Speeds things up considerable.

William I meant – to take the body. And bury you.

Sarah Not in this parish. Or if I have I've forgotten 'em. (*Pause.*) Another life. Like a dream now. (*Pause.*) They'll have me on the butcher's slab and set to with the chopper. I'll be splayed out there like a lump of meat, I'll have no defence, clamp me knees together they'll chop 'em off, slice my thighs to rashers, and there's my honour up for grabs. And off with her hands. And off with her noisy old head. And now I am dismembered by a dozen men, me giblets all over the floor, and they have their leathery fingers in me in the name of science, searching for the bit that went bad.

William (*aghast*) How can you talk like that?

Sarah How? Damn, if I got to think it, every other bugger will too.

William . . . I don't half pity you.

Sarah You after the bad bit, too? That what you come here to paint? The evil, the rot, and that?

William Well, I'm just doing a sketch.

Sarah I can throw a fit if you like.

William (*interested*) Oh? What sort of a fit?

Sarah I don't know, a mad fit. (*She rolls her eyes.*)

William And what's the effect of that?

Sarah Scares the shite out of magistrates, mainly. (*Laughs. Subsides.*) Something bubbles up inside me, I don't know.

William (*disapproving*) But we all have these urges, and we all have to contain them.

Sarah Why?

William Don't ask stupid questions, it's bleeding obvious, isn't it?

Sarah Why?

William Well – for fear of what the law will do to us otherwise!

Sarah But I am a law to myself. Now. The judges have run out of punishments.

William Oh, Christ, how can you argue against it? – You have to have respect for the law, Sarah.

Sarah You're not getting fucking hung in the morning. – How is it out, is it wet?

William It's windy, with the last of an autumn sun.

Sarah I bet it rains tomorrow then. Now, I shall sit like a proper lady so's you feel at your ease. I want you to do your best work. You can imagine for yourself the lapdog and the velvet and the little negro feller with the studded silver collar and you can put them in when you get back home. Just get the essence of me for now. (*Pause.*) I'll sit as still as still. (*Pause.*) Like I sat after I done the killings. Ever so peaceful. Not thinking no more. Calm as a duck on a pond. God there is such relief in murder . . .! (*Pause.*) The dogs stop baying in your head. – I ain't alarming you, am I, Mr Hogarth, you seem to have stopped . . .?

William Yes, you are, slightly.

Sarah Why, whatever sort of a person do you think I am?

William You're a murderess.

Sarah Oh, that. I have my better side. Jesus, I wasn't born killing.

Without warning, she gets up, hoists her skirts, and squats over a bucket.

William Oi!

Sarah What?

William What the fuck are you playing at? (*He looks closely.*)

Sarah Won't be a tic.

William That's indecent, a woman piddling in public.

Sarah I don't care.

William That's obscene.

Sarah All done now. (*She resumes her pose at the table.*)

William . . . Haven't you got no shame?

Sarah It's a blank, it's all a blank. Decency, dignity, pride. A sour piss in a rusty bucket. From the moment I picked up the razor. To the moment my feet swing through the air. A blank. Get drawing, then, it's getting dark.

William I hate despair, I really do.

Sarah I ain't despairing. It's just all one to me. This world, it don't change. I just don't fight against it no more. – Here, what you got in that basket?

William That's for later.

Sarah What's for later? Is it me food?

William Do you want your picture taken down or not?

Sarah I want to know why a famous high society painter wants to do a portrait of silly old me.

William Well, I'm recently married, I need the cash.

Sarah Why you bothering with me, then? I haven't got none.

William It's business, that's all. I'm a businessman.

Sarah And I thought you were an artist.

William I'm an artist who likes to eat.

Sarah What've you brung me? What?

William So you *can* be tempted . . . Something in you stirs . . .

Sarah It's me belly, it's going mad!

William Let's finish the sketch first, shall we? Then eat?

Sarah I'm destroyed with hunger, root and branch I wither, look at me droop, me neck'll be slipping out the noose at this rate and you'll be to blame, go on, give us a crust to chew on while you're working.

William No, you wouldn't keep still.

Sarah groans.

I haven't got for ever, have I? It's not as if I can come back next week and re-do your great chomping gob!

Sarah stands.

I'm sorry, I'm sorry –

Sarah goes to a dark corner of the cell.

Where exactly do you think you're off to?

Sarah I can get out of the light, at least.

William But you made your mark on a legal paper. Your consent.

Sarah Don't mean a thing to me. I can't read.

William Look, do you want your place in fucking history or don't you?

Sarah I am about to die, I think I am entitled to a bite to eat!

William (*considers the situation*) Miss . . . 'Sorry' is a remarkable word, isn't it? In the few months I've lived with my wife I've begun to see the value of it. Every little petty quarrel can be sorted. Jane tries to make me see the female point of view. I would have said to ask forgiveness was unmanly. My fists were permanently clenched. My jaw thrust in to any barney. But now I can be meek as a bleeding lamb when the need arises. Give me two more minutes. Please. You did make your cross!

Sarah (*suddenly returns*) Well! Who is this woman who can work such wonders?

William Her father is Serjeant-Painter to the King.

Sarah Oh, married the boss's daughter.

William Don't be so cheeky.

Sarah I see now how you got in with the nobs.

William I did not marry for reasons of commerce. I married for love. However I do have a new series of paintings on view at my house, inspired by some ideas of my wife's, which I've reason to believe may make me a fortune.

Sarah Why've you come here then?

William You are notorious. I think there may be a quick profit in it. I have a lot of debts.

Sarah (*smiles*) . . . As long as people see that I am bad.
I want to be bad. That's how I want to be remembered.
As an insult. A spit in the face. Do me like that.

William nods.

I could kill you for the food, I s'pose . . . But I can't be
bothered. Not after I just had a wash.

They both resume their seats.

William Christ, what a day. (*He draws.*)

Sarah A blunt razor I used to kill the old women. The
widow's memento of her long-dead man. I was that
ravenous, I had ceased to think, and that felt good, you
can think too much when you're starving. I knew that
my mistress's treasure was under her cot. So I bled the
bitch and her bedmate while they slept. (*Laughs.*) Two
stuck pigs in their petticoats. The rage, the urge to eat
crept over me, and I succumbed. The peacefulest
moment I ever have known . . . that second I abandoned
trying to be good. You throw off the wretched, useless
rags you've gone cold in all your life – the common
sense, the reason – throw it to the wind and go naked,
raw, free suddenly . . . Then Mary, the maid, with who
I shared the attic, appeared on the stair, so I had to kill
her too – aren't you done yet?

*William is sitting with his chalk held in mid-air. Then
he scrawls on the bottom of the paper, and is finished.*

William (*quiet*) The two old women, yes, I kind of
understand, I read that they mistreated you . . . but the
maid? Why the maid? Why on earth?

Sarah Shrieked at the blood, soppy cow. I knew that if
I was committing the perfect crime I could scarce afford
to leave a witness.

William . . . Why'd you get caught then?

Sarah Ah. Don't know. I can't explain things. Not in words. I never even managed to sell the damn silver. So hunger follows me down to the lime-pit.

William (*sickened*) Women killing women . . .

Sarah Don't men kill men? – Can I have a look, then?

Wearily, William puts his sketch in front of her. He takes a bottle of beer from the basket and drinks.

William Understand, it's not finished, it's only a rough –

Sarah Me?

William I'll work it up in the studio, oh sod, I hate it the first time they –

Sarah That – is me?

William That is a – preliminary version of you.

Sarah takes out her spoon, polishes it, stares at the picture, stares at her reflection, stares at the picture again.

Sarah It's warped.

William No, the spoon's warped, the spoon distorts –

Sarah That's a good silver spoon! Are you telling me I look like that?

William I'm not completely useless with a stick of chalk.

Sarah Liar!

William What's this, criticism?

Sarah Look at her with the little pout and the sparkle in the corner of her eye. The face is hard but. But! Do I ever sit like that with my damn knees apart? I do not. You give me desire. I have none!

William It's the best I could manage.

Sarah But the whole blasted reason I'm in here in the first place is that I would not whore! And you gone and made me one! Oh, there's plenty of room in the brothels for hungry farm-girls, plenty of quick shillings to be earned in cold and dingy courtyards, but would I descend to it? – no, I had my respect, dullwit I now see myself to be, I lived like a beast but I wouldn't sell *that*!

William My head is throbbing, will you pipe down? I must say in my defence it said in the newspapers that –

Sarah The newspapers are the main reason I have never bothered to learn to read.

William You are described as a laundress.

Sarah Possibly because I am one.

William But you can't make a living as a laundress, can you? Too many people are content to go dirty.

Sarah But I've a right to a reputation like anyone else!

William Look, I'm an artist, an artist must be free to view the world unhindered.

Sarah Why?

William Well, he can't let his subjects dictate to him!

Sarah Why not?

William Christ you're impossible.

Sarah You have made me some creation of your own. Warped what you see sitting here. You assumed. You are a prick. And what's this squiggle at the bottom?

William (*picks up sketch*) That? Oh, that's my signature. So people know it's authentic. (*Explains.*) By me.

Sarah . . . What people?

William The ones who'll come to look when I exhibit the finished painting.

Sarah Where?

William In my house in Covent Garden.

Sarah Never. I want it destroyed.

William Oh, please don't be difficult.

Sarah You got me mad now.

William It's just one bloody thing after another. (*He gathers his things up.*)

Sarah It's not how I want to go down! In the future! I told you, I want to look evil, I feel evil, I got demons in me and where are they in this balls-up? I want to be bad! Through and through! Not fallen angel! Not mildewed rose! Now give it back!

William I am truly sorry, Sarah, but it's mine, I own it, I hold a thing called the copyright you see. I must be going now. I have a pressing appointment. Why don't you help yourself to supper?

He hammers on the door. It's quite dark in the cell now.

Sarah It is my picture. *My* picture. Picture of *me*.

William (*calls*) William Hogarth! Open up!

Sarah (*calm*) Give me my likeness back, you are stealing it, you are taking my soul.

William Sarah . . . Believe me . . . I am so sorry for you.

A horrible wailing noise, the screaming of women, very loud. William clutches at his head. Sarah is still.

Oh . . .! What's that?

*Suddenly, from the shadows in the corners of the cell,
a number of nightmarish women prisoners emerge and
run at William. They clutch at him. He tries to get
away, yelling for the Gaoler. All the time this dreadful
noise, half-pain, half-laughter. Sarah remains still. The
cell door clangs open. The Gaoler stands brandishing
his whip. The prisoners, except Sarah, disappear.
William runs out with the picture. Sarah falls on the
basket and stuffs food into her mouth. She bends over,
retching. The Gaoler goes up to her.*

Gaoler Here, love, you all right? What's the matter, can't
your stomach take it?

*Sarah comes up in a swift movement and gets her arm
round the Gaoler's neck. Her other hand comes up
from the basket with a small knife in it. She slits his
throat. He falls and dies.*

Sarah Mad I said. Good and mad.

She picks up the Gaoler's bunch of keys. Blackout.

SCENE FOUR

*Louisa's lodging. William is asleep, sprawled in a chair,
a glass of red wine clutched in his lap and tilting
dangerously. Louisa enters, taking off her shawl. She
sees him. She groans inwardly. She goes to him and
removes his wig from his head. He mutters in his sleep.*

William The faces . . . Those faces . . .

*Louisa smoothes his cropped hair. She tries to take the
glass out of his hand but he won't let go. She kneels in
front of him and starts to prise his fingers open. He*

*hangs on so tightly that he wakes up. Seeing Louisa
kneeling between his legs, he fears the worst. He leaps
away in panic.*

What, again? Why can't you leave me alone?

Louisa You were spilling your drink.

William Lou . . .? Louisa? Is it you? Am I awake?

Louisa You were dreaming. Your eyes flicking back and
forth beneath the lids. Like a lizard on a pebble.

William Had to come. Couldn't keep away no longer.

Louisa (*sighs*) I've only just knocked off work.

William I've had a pig of a day and all. I've been locked
up in Newgate Gaol. I'm doing a print of Sarah
Sprackling. (*He has it rolled up in his pocket.*) Plan to
have an edition on sale straight after the poor woman's
turned off. Get in while she's still fresh in the public
imagination – all those crowds who will bay at the
hanging – last portrait of the deceased – got to be an
earner. So I went down to her dungeon to sketch a
design for the engraving and I – I can't describe them,
there were these females – they come at me and – their
faces! The eyes of them!

Louisa Sit down, Will.

William Feels like the seams are splitting in my head, the
skin tight on the skull . . .!

Louisa Let Louisa make it better. (*She cradles his head.*)

William The dreams are bad enough, but waking visions –
Christ!

Louisa You can always come to me, you know that.

William I know I can, Lou, I haven't been since the
wedding because I –

Louisa Don't have to explain. I understand.

William You do, I know you do.

Pause.

Louisa What's her father like? The Serjeant-Painter?

William Oh, you know who she is, then?

Louisa Well, today was the first time we'd been formally introduced, but I like to keep myself in the picture, yes.

William He's not a bad bloke. We have a natter up the scaffold in St Paul's – he's doing the inside of the dome. We get along all right, but I don't feel I'm in the presence of a fellow-genius, if you know what I mean.

Louisa I know what you mean.

William Not everyone does.

Louisa You're not very happy, dear, are you?

William No I'm not. I know I ought to be. That makes it worse.

Louisa Do you talk to anyone else about it?

William Who for example?

Louisa I don't know. Your friends?

William I haven't got any. I have allies, yes. I don't have friends.

Louisa Well, what about the wife? Can't you confide in her? I thought that's what they were for, baring of the soul and what have you. – No?

William Well, she's young, isn't she, she's a lot younger than you or me, mate, there are things I wouldn't want to burden her with, seeing she's –

Louisa You mean she doesn't know about –

William – a respectable girl from a good background who –

Louisa – how you like your lover to –

William – is deeply in love with me and –

Louisa – piss and shit in your –

William Well of course not, she's my wife! I stood up with her in a bleeding church, I can't ask her to do that! She's a decent, well-bred girl!

Louisa Then presumably she doesn't push her finger in your bottom when you –

William No she doesn't, of course she doesn't, she wouldn't know where to start!

Louisa So we're not completely satisfied with married life . . .?

William Not completely, no!

Louisa Husbands . . . Out there in the world you seem so capable, on top of things, the man in the saddle. But in my dingy bedroom . . . the dark, wild longings . . . stampede of forbidden desires . . . secret needs which you'll only admit –

William Oh, the sex in my dreams!

Louisa – to your whore.

William My erections in the dead of night, dear Christ, like wood, like stone!

Louisa Sometimes I think I understand men. What a mistake that is. A woman will talk to another woman about what gives her pleasure. In this trade, we have to work at it if we want anything for ourselves, so we swap ideas, trying to . . . remember . . . – But the way you lot carry on you'd think it was against the law to admit you'd got your dick up. Probably is, come to think of it.

William Listen, I had this dream –

Louisa You are paying the going rate, are you, Will?

William What, after all these years?

Louisa Yes.

William Jesus. – A little old woman was sucking me off –

Louisa What?

William A little old woman was sucking me off –

Louisa Is this a dream or a nursery rhyme?

William A little old lady, yes, I thought it repulsive at first but then I got to quite enjoy it. But then it turned – my whatsit – turned into this kind of brittle, burnt-up sausage effort, and it broke off in her mouth, all flaky and crumbly, and she munched away at it until it was gone. Completely gone! I looked down to see if another one was growing. At first I had only a bit of a stump. Fuck, I thought, that's the last time I'm unfaithful. But then I saw I had a little winkle like a little boy's. It was growing back. I was turning into some kind of reptile.

Louisa (*laughs*) Perhaps that means you've got a hidden fear of –

William Don't try and interpret it! I'm not interested in interpreting it! I'm interested in making it go away! – Another time I was making love with a man. And I enjoyed it. In the dream. How am I supposed to explain all this to Jane? She thinks I'm a great painter. She thinks I'm an idealist!

Louisa Someone ought to put her straight.

William Well, that's not very friendly.

Louisa And why should I be? Once, way back in the mists of time, you spoke love, whispered love . . .

William (*quiet*) Heat of the moment, darling.

Louisa Thought I was getting out of it . . . New life dawning and all that bunk.

A drum roll, off.

Drummer (*off*) Announcing, tonight at the Haymarket, at prices to suit every pocket –

William Oh God. Harry's play.

Drummer (*off*) A brand new farce by Mr Henry Fielding!

A parade enters and marches round the auditorium. It comprises a Woman Drummer, wearing a fancy bonnet and a flowing skirt, and beating a large drum which sways on her hip; Harry Fielding, separated from the main group; Oliver; Frank; Mrs Needham; and a Man in a comic mask from a masquerade. Louisa and William look out at the procession, but the marchers do not acknowledge them.

Harry A dozen years? Fifteen? How long has the bastard been in power? How long will you stand for it?

William Christ, he's pissed as a rat.

Harry Butterfly-like he flits from crown to crown, with his tongue in the nation's honey!

Louisa He'll get himself arrested.

William It's pathetic. Why can't he face up to reality? Oh, you can make a big noise, let all the world know how radical you are, but then down comes the polished boot of power – prevents you from doing your work!

Louisa You don't have to justify yourself to me.

Harry Listen to this catalogue of corruption: 'First Lord of the Treasury, Mr Walpole. First Lord of the Admiralty, Mr Walpole. Clerk of the Pells, Mr Walpole's son. Customs of London, second son of Mr Walpole.'

William But in my silence I am eloquent you see. I keep on turning it out.

Harry 'Secretary to the Treasury, Mr Walpole's brother. Postmaster General, Mr Walpole's other brother. Secretary to Ireland, another brother of Mr double-damned Walpole! Secretary to the Postmaster General, Mr shit-head Walpole's shag-wit brother-in-law!'

Louisa I told you, it doesn't matter, I'm just a worn-out old jade.

Harry It's disease at the heart of the state!

William No, Louisa, sweetheart, sweetheart, you're much more than that.

Harry He's like a man who poisons a fountain from which everyone must drink!

William Just ignore him, maybe he'll go away.

Harry Are you all deaf? Are you all blind? Or do you just choose not to look?

Louisa Will – is it true you put me in a set of drawings?

William (*defensive*) Everyone always thinks it's *them* I've used for a model.

Louisa I have no illusions. I only wondered. What could I do about it if you had?

William I want you to do what you know that I like.

Louisa I'm right at the bottom and on the way down.

William Fart for me. Go on, Lou. Fart in my face, Lou. Please.

Louisa Oh, Willy . . .

With a sigh Louisa lifts her skirt and William disappears underneath. He is completely hidden. The parade floods onto the stage. Louisa stares straight ahead, sad, unseeing.

Harry It's so dark . . . So bleak . . . How long till dawn?

Harry slumps. Oliver, with bottle in hand, approaches Louisa. He squeezes her breast. She does not respond.

Frank Look at him, he's on the go again already, the dog, and barely an hour since we left your house.

Mrs Needham I had to get him away, Frank. He was killing her. The Viscount's underclothes are caked with blood.

Oliver (*leaves Louisa*) Slack like a fish washed up on the beach. Not sure if one can be bothered.

Drummer Performance begins in fifteen minutes! Good seats still to be had!

They all prepare to move off. The Man in the mask beckons Frank aside, away from Harry.

Man Frank? 'Tis Frank, isn't it? – A word with you.

The Man lowers his mask. It is Walpole. Frank is stunned and frightened.

Frank Sir . . .! Christ.

Louisa senses something.

Louisa What's that?

A noise of howling wind. They all look around,
uncertain.

Mrs Needham Where?

Suddenly Sarah passes through them at great speed,
skipping, dancing across the stage, her knife flashing
close to throats and wrists and genitals, a manic
Samurai in rags. As quickly as she came, she is gone.
A stunned pause. A blackout. Then Mrs Needham
screams.

SCENE FIVE

The Hogarths' house. A large bed. Moonlight coming
through a window. Flickering shadows from candles in
corners. Jane is in her nightclothes, brushing her hair.

Jane Listen, my hair crackles with desire. Why don't you
come home? William? I would do now what you wanted
in the park. I just must be private, it is my nature. Under
my sheets I will do anything, nothing's too dirty for my
little man. He will come a million times. His heart will
burst from coming.

She looks out of the window.

This is all assuming he gets home within the next five
minutes, because otherwise, forget it, I'm not that
devoted to the idea.

She gets into bed and blows out her candle.

His hands! I can't rid my thoughts of his hands. Stubby
fingers exploring the bones in my back, grimy nails that
rasp on silk, slipping, sliding, tumbling down my grassy
slopes . . . We lie for hours, twined like rope, like vines,
all licks and dribbles, tooth on grape, inner thigh –

Silent and unseen, Sarah enters, and listens.

– on inner thigh, he calls it the Line of Beauty, perpetual spiral of perfect art – we lose our limbs, begin to blend – we become snakes, we slither together – our flicking tongues – oh William –

Sarah knocks against something. Jane sits up.

Will? What are you –

Sarah leaps on to the bed and puts the knife to Jane's throat.

Sarah It's a cheese knife. Recognise it? I fancy it come from your kitchen. Not a murmur now or I take the rind off you. I gather from your whimpering that Willy is not home yet . . .? Then I shall have to wait, shan't I.

Jane What do you want? Money? I deal with the money in this house.

Sarah No, I don't want your money, what would I want with money? Unlike every other beggar in the world, I can not be purchased. My name is Sarah Sprackling.

Jane gasps.

Oh good, someone's heard of me. Your husband came to see me in my cell, down in the sump of human sewage, promising to do my picture.

Jane Didn't he do it?

Sarah Oh, he done it –

Jane He keeps his word.

Sarah – but I don't like it.

Jane Ah.

Sarah I want it back. And if he won't give it I'll kill him.

Jane Do you think that will be absolutely necessary?

A commotion outside in the hallway. The voices of Robert Walpole and a servant.

Servant (*off*) No, sir, you can't go in there, that's My Lady's bedroom!

Walpole (*off*) I goes where I damn well wants.

Sarah (*knife*) Hide me.

Jane Under the blankets! There's nowhere else.

Walpole (*off*) Matter of state security, this is.

She hides in the bed next to Jane. Walpole blusters in. Jane pretends to be waking up.

Jane Oh, what a horrid dream . . .

Walpole Mrs Hogarth? Is that you?

Jane Who is it?

Walpole My name is Robert Walpole. Please forgive the indiscretion.

Jane Mr Walpole!

Walpole I must speak to your husband. Where is he?

Jane I don't know. Is he in trouble?

Walpole He will be if he's not careful. You know this prostitute thing? This 'Harlot's Progress'?

Jane Well what do you think? It is on easels in the drawing room.

Walpole There is a rumour, madam, there is a nasty little worm of a rumour wriggling through town. It slithered up to me only this evening, and whispered, through a mouth of slime, that William's planning a follow-up – based on me.

Jane 'Sir Robert Walpole's Progress'?

Walpole It doesn't have that ring, does it, that poetry, it lacks a certain something, do try and put him off. Mrs Hogarth, your husband is a genius. But he is no politician. He is like a child out there in the big world, away from his brush and palette. And I am very conscious of my somewhat battered public image. After all he is beholden to me, on account of the Salver.

Jane Salver? What Salver?

Walpole Hasn't he told you of the bond between us?

Jane He's always said he was an independent artist!

Walpole There is no such thing. Madam, a history lesson, very brief. Perhaps you know that on the demise of the monarch the Great Seal of England has to he redesigned, and it is the honour and duty of the Chancellor of the Exchequer, who by some accident, at the sad death of His Majesty George the First, happened to be me, to convert the old matrix into a memorial silver plate. Now Chancellors of the Exchequer do not as a rule survive the turmoil of an incoming reign, having usually made a fiscal bollocks of the preceding one, but by some fluke it chanced to be me who took delivery of His Majesty George the Second's spanking brand new Seal. Then I sets about getting an engraver for me plate.

Jane A silver engraver.

Walpole Oh, you've a sharp mind for a woman in her nightie. Some vicious satires he had done. The Royal Family scorned! You have no idea how the laughter of the illiterate rings in the halls of St James's. Put your satires in books, by all means, 'Gulliver's Travels', yes yes yes, the Queen enjoys a read – but pictures? Everyone will get it! Worse than bloody plays! Can you imagine –

a picture in every home? Your hubby-to-be was sailing into danger. I could hardly allow such influence to rest in the hands of an artist. I had to help him to the safe high ground of creative endeavour – the oil painting. But how to bung him up there without denting his pride? Blinding flash of inspiration, commissioned him to engrave the Walpole Salver. Lovely job he did, too, old Hercules putting the allegorical screws on Calumny and Envy. A charming introduction into the bosom of polite society, and with it the opportunity to make enough to marry. Always chuffed to help a genius earn a shilling. But he is my man now, and damned if I let him forget it.

There is a burst of angry laughter from beneath the bedclothes. Walpole pulls them back to discover Sarah.

And now I am embarrassed. I thought it might have been the genius. In hiding. Wrath of the gods et cetera et cetera.

Jane My friend is keeping me company whilst my husband is out.

Walpole And devilishly pleasant company, too, if a wee bit of an urchin.

Jane The noise in the hallway . . . she snuggled down . . . I will give my husband your message, Mr Walpole. If that is all? We are very tired.

Walpole Yes. No. (*He drops a purse on the bed.*) Twenty guineas. If you – do it. Now. In front of me. I burn with curiosity, it is something I have always desired to watch. How exactly do you manage to –

Jane How dare you! Please leave at once.

Walpole Very well. Pity.

Walpole picks up his money and turns to leave. Sarah takes Jane's chin in her hand and plants a long, hard kiss on her mouth. Walpole gapes. He takes the money from his pocket again. But when he does so, Sarah abruptly breaks off the kiss and shouts at him.

Sarah What do you think we are?

Walpole A brace of bitches. (*He pockets his money and exits.*)

Sarah More money than I ever seen . . . But they would make bed just like gaol. Have you ever noticed how they love the thought of women having women, but hate to think of men seducing men?

Jane That was the Prime Minister that you just made a fool of.

Sarah Well? Who's he going to tell? The Queen?

They fall into a fit of giggles, unable to contain themselves, letting out their tension. Then Jane stops laughing.

Jane What do you want here? Why don't you just go away and leave us in peace?

A distant bell tolls midnight.

Sarah This is the start of my last day on earth. Why should I leave you in peace?

Her knife-blade glints in the moonlight. Slow fade.

Act Two

Drury Lane, the same night. A dog barks in the distance. William stands wrapped in a white sheet in the middle of the road.

William I don't feel powerful. Naked like this. I don't feel like a bloke who takes advantage. Look at me, I stand here in a state of droop. Authority has been sucked and squirted from me like the juice from a Spanish orange. How can I be a tyrant? I am a deliberate weakling. My little foot is on nobody's throat! Look!

Louisa appears at a window above, half-dressed.

Louisa You're a bastard, you're all bastards.

William Men will be bastards, granted, yes, the evidence is overwhelming, but I'm sorry I refuse to accept complicity in every bloody crime of the sex. I am trying hard to rise above it. I have the greatest respect for womankind. I simply happen to have come out without any bloody money.

Louisa You are an exploitative bastard, Will! Like all men you try and turn every defeat to your own advantage.

William Oh, do me a favour! It's you! You, wanting payment for a thing that should be free. Simple human loving, and you present me with a bill. Christ, the avarice of this city . . .

Louisa You can't accept your imperfection, so you unload it on to me. You foul and you defile me, then claim it's you that's abused. It's always the same.

William Do I have to stand here and listen to this shit?

Louisa Looks like it, doesn't it?

William Fucking cunt!

Louisa Then you turn violent. And out comes the language. It's always the same. Viciousness tempered with guilt.

William All I want is my clothes back, Louisa.

Louisa Then pay what you owe.

William Oh come on, darling, I thought we was friends.

Louisa Friends! Is this any way to treat your friends?

William I only asked if I could put it on the slate.

Louisa You can put it on the stove and boil it, chum, before you put it anywhere near me again. (*Exits.*)

William Lou! (*Pause.*) What a slag, honestly . . . A mercenary on the battlefields of desire. Wading through acres of red genitalia, breast bared, hips flying, and hand stretched out for her ruthless shilling. – O pity the poor debtors! They are the wretched of the earth.

Louisa reappears above. He doesn't see her.

All this for a moment's peace, in her, one second of perfection, one fleeting glimpse of beauty, when the universe drops its knickers and puts everything on view . . . simple, simple, it's all so simple . . . Then back comes chaos crashing in. Back to the body and the bartering for warmth. Thinking, does she see this apparition too – or is she, as seems highly likely, conning?

Louisa You are so self-important, William Hogarth, so puffed up, I don't know how you survive the sheer ordinariness of life, never mind draw it. 'One second of perfection'! Talk about seeing things from a male point of view! You have to learn not to piss on your mates. You can't just use people for your own purposes and then abandon them.

William I never abandoned no one. – I've come back, haven't I?

Louisa You drive me round the twist, you do! You drive me bloody barmy! I should have shopped you to your pure-arsed wife.

William Yeh, all right, but what about my clothes?

Louisa Might get a few bob for them, I suppose. I don't want you to freeze to death, however –

William You're right, it's bitter, open the door.

Louisa – so you can have this back, it's no fucking use to me.

She throws his wig out. It wafts to the ground.
William puts it on his head and strides about, huffing.

William Oh, thank you very much, my precious! Thank you very, very much! At least now I can walk the streets with dignity! At least I won't be taken for a twat!

Louisa Good night. (*Exits.*)

William seethes. Then he sniffs and wipes his nose on the sheet. Then he seethes again.

William I have a sword, you know. Gentleman of leisure I may not be but I have bought myself a blade – saved for it for bloody years and never used the fucker! Shall I try it on your flaccid skin for sharpness?

Unseen, Harry enters, drunk, with bottle. He watches William from a distance.

Yes, I like the thought! I shall chamfer my initials on your droopy old tits, and on your bum engrave the crosshatch of my vengeance! You have gone too bloody far my girl.

He turns to leave and sees Harry.

Wotcher, Harry.

Harry Hello, Will.

William Yes, well . . .

Harry You wouldn't, would you?

William What?

Harry All that carving and slashing.

William (*jaw thrust out*) I might.

Harry Seriously?

William I might!

Harry Why?

William She done me a mischief.

Harry I see. Well, we've all got it in us.

William She nicked my clothes!

Harry And for that, you want to cut her up?

William Fucking do, mate. Fucking make me feel a fucking lot better.

Pause. Harry watches him. He breaks.

Of course I don't, she's a friend of mine, what do you think I am, a maniac?

Harry Why'd you say it, then?

William I didn't bloody mean it, did I!

Harry It's easy to over-react. After you've hired a woman. One wrong word and you could kill. You've been turfed out, have you?

William All because I forgot to bring my money with me. I ask you.

Harry Will, you have never been known to forget your money. The precise whereabouts and condition of your purse is invariably the thought uppermost in your mind.

William Yes, well, thing is, I'm skint.

Harry Then why go to a tart? It's asking for trouble.

William . . . I'm in love.

Harry How does it feel?

William It hurts.

Harry The heart will ache, it is traditional.

William Not the heart. My balls.

Harry Have you tried explaining your feelings to the object of your affections? (*He indicates the house behind.*)

William What? – No, no, no, I'm not in love with her! She's a prostitute! Christ!

Harry Then who – ?

William Why, I'm in love with my wife, of course!

Harry Sorry, my mistake.

William I fucking worship her, Harry. She is my life. The blood in my veins.

Harry Forgive my abject stupidity, will you, it is the alcohol has paralysed my brains, but just tell me why in that case you come down Drury Lane of a midnight?

William I want my wife to respect me. I have these impulses, you see, and I – oh, fuck, what's it got to do with you? (*He turns away. He turns back.*) Jane has certain expectations of me, right? Naturally I want to live up to them.

Harry But you sometimes need a break from being perfect.

William Yes! Need relief. Any man would.

Harry And, er –

William Louisa, yes –

Harry Does a very good job I bet.

William Hmm. – Here, how did you get on at Mrs Needham's?

Harry I don't want to talk about it. Change the subject.

Pause. They sit drinking in the gutter. Suddenly Harry breaks down.

Oh, Will, the bad taste of this town . . .

William It's as old as the wind. The disappointment after.

Harry It's not disappointment, I was not disappointed! But how could I enjoy it? I, a man of letters? A poet, dipped in that pot of flesh? Oh I got so angry with myself! The things I made the creature do . . . The worst of it all was she took it all for normal. Peggy. My bollocks adrift in her oceans of fat . . . Her weak eyes blank like bedsheets . . .

William Don't get upset.

Harry Always been in love before. Always been passionate. Union of spirits. This was like coming in a corpse.

William Harry, it's not important.

Harry (*snuffles*) To me it is, I think it's important to admit, to recognise, what we are capable of. Because it's so alarming.

William Look, will you please not cry, I can't stand to see a man cry. It's a tough old life I know, but . . . (*Gently.*) Harry . . .

> *William tries to comfort Harry without actually touching him. He offers him the bottle.*

Harry We alter the world around us but we never change ourselves inside. We hear the first rumbles of industrial progress but what will it bring us? Will it make us happy? Or will we sink deeper and deeper into the web of our own stupidity? Look at the people we allow to govern us, for God's sake! Are they working for the common good?

William Well, nobody's perfect.

Harry But you can't just leave it at that!

William I love human beings for their failures. It's the only way I can live with myself.

Harry Why won't you listen to what I'm bloody saying?

William Because you go in so hard. Everything you do is an act of aggression. Art should also celebrate. Or it does not tell the truth.

Harry No, no, it should abuse, it should insult, the audience should be shocked, disturbed, and made to think again!

William Don't be a berk. They love to be shocked! They love it! They take it as proof of their own broadminded-ness! It doesn't alter a bleeding thing. You have to work gently, cleverly, bit by bit . . .

Harry No, it's just that I'm not good enough. Not hard enough. A truly oppositional ideal will outrage the most unshockable of palates.

William Oh fucking hell.

Harry I have not found it. I make too many jokes. This evening they laughed and laughed. The bastards.

William . . . Well, it was a comedy, wasn't it?

Harry England in the 1730s? A comedy?

William But Christ, if it's *funny* –

Harry Well of course it's funny, you've got to mock or you might as well curl up and die! But satire is too sugary, too easy to swallow. I dream of writing something where the laughs turn into tears. Where the wit is sharp like a mouthful of lemon. The truth is not a joke. It's dark. The only light is love, the only thing that redeems us, salvages us from the world we have made. And what do we do? We betray it.

William But what do you want? People to suddenly metamorphose overnight into some better kind of being?

Harry Less than a hundred years ago these same people executed the King! Never forget that. Nothing is impossible.

William But there's no point swimming against the tide! It's daft! What I'm gonna do is, I'm gonna do a set of prints that'll be dirt cheap to buy, right, I mean fuck, I don't care if you wrap your fish in them, but what I'm thinking of Harry is this: they'll infiltrate. My modern moral subjects. They'll sneak into peoples' homes – ordinary people – and creep up on to the walls and they'll hang over the bedsteads and they'll niggle. They'll take on the old prejudices and they'll worry them by the throat . . . they won't sicken, but they'll nag . . .

Harry In an amusing sort of way.

William In an amusing sort of way.

Harry You just want the loot.

William I've gone so long without it, I do have rather a lust for the stuff.

Harry As an artist, William, you're a coward. You will not point your finger.

William To point your finger, Henry, you must first remove it from your arse. I admire what you write but you talk like a turd. The simple truth is, Walpole exists. He is power. I believe in the reality of power. It is a tangible thing. If power chooses to censor, then censor it will. He'll have you by the nuts, mate. You want to keep an eye on the little shrinkers.

Harry Don't patronise me. I thought you were ambitious.

William I am ambitious.

Harry But not for change. For yourself, but not for others. Not to bring down Walpole.

William Bring down this Walpole, up pops another Walpole.

Harry It's almost as if the satirist needs a sick society . . . has a vested interest in preserving it . . . so you can feed off it . . . suck its blood . . .

William I just want to survive. That is my ambition. Have another drink.

Harry No. No more drinks.

> *A sedan chair with drawn curtains is carried on by two chairmen. They set it down and open it up. Walpole steps out.*

Walpole Mr Fielding. Mr Hogarth. In fancy dress. Shared bottle of gin. Jolly good.

William Servant sir.

Harry Sir.

Walpole So glad I've managed to find you at last, William. I have just paid a courtesy call on your charming wife. I didn't know she was a lesbian.

William She's not.

Walpole She's not, she's not, what am I saying, how could she possibly be? Married to a chap like yourself. She must just have been experimenting. We all do when we are young. But when we grow up we find we want to settle down. Oh, we do, Henry, we do. We discover that what we want most, what gives us the greatest pleasure and the greatest freedom to enjoy it, is stability. The ship of state on an even keel. No danger to the cargo. Oh, heaving and rolling with the natural swell, perhaps, but the captain in full command. By some strange quirk of fate I have ended up at the helm, lashed to the wheel of this glorious boat. And I have steered her on to a course of peace and prosperity. Because peace is the perfect condition for trade, and trade will make us rich, and rich is what we want to be, correct? Fifty thousand men slain this year on the fields of Europe, and not one of them English! How proud I am of that. (*Pause.*) Or would you prefer a hunting metaphor? Gentlemen? I am a hunting man. Across the stubbly fields of Norfolk, I hunt, foxes or women, don't mind which. Backside raw in the saddle, horse at a furious gallop, naked lady making for the woods, my idea of heaven. However it would be positively no trouble at all to me to set my hounds on the scent of meddlesome artists. Wherever you go, into what ditch, behind what copse, through what fields of swaying barley I will hunt you down and dip my finger in your blood and smear it in triumph on the nearest child's face. (*To Harry.*) Metaphorically speaking, of course, this is all part of the same extended conceit, as I'm sure you recognise. I have some literary aspirations myself, you see.

Harry I wouldn't count on overnight success if I were you.

Walpole Success may not be what I'm after, boy. – I believe it will one day become the mark of a cultured society, that its artistic members realise when they have gone too far, and voluntarily apply the curb. It is a struggle, self-restraint, dear me yes – but think of the rewards.

Harry What are they exactly?

Walpole Well, I shan't have to raid your theatre and charge all the actors under the vagrancy laws, as I did shortly after the final curtain this evening.

Harry Oh, not again! Why?

Walpole The play was offensive. Public sensibilities were offended.

Harry How do you know? You weren't even there!

Walpole I will pass over the unkind satirical jibes at myself, for the age cries out for satire, they say. Which must mean the age is pretty damn sure of itself. But I hear, sir, that you are preparing yet another scurrilous item.

Harry It's going to be called *The Historical Register* – a political calendar of the year – all four seasons of your mould and decay.

Walpole Don't proceed with it. Or I shall be forced to introduce a censor's office.

Harry You can't.

Walpole I was thinking of giving the job to the Lord Chamberlain.

Harry You can't!

William Don't push your luck, mate.

Harry Parliament will never approve it!

Walpole Shut up. (*To William.*) You're toying with the idea of another 'Progress' series, are you?

William I think you must be misinformed.

Walpole Good, I don't like progress, I like things as they are.

Harry I should like to know your constitutional –

Walpole Will you be quiet.

Harry This is a free country, sir! I am a freeborn Englishman, and I have a right to speak!

Walpole Oh, do grow up, Henry.

Harry Go on, then! Do it! Do it, if you dare!

Walpole You've gone all red.

Harry I was just thinking, when you burn your boats, what a bloody good fire it makes! (*Exits, angrily.*)

William (*defending Harry*) He's had a bad day.

Walpole Why? The play was a triumph. Why are you chaps so perverse? (*Pause. He sits and drinks from the gin bottle.*) My houses are stuffed full of art, you know. It's such a damned good investment. I got a Titian last year for two pounds ten. It's already worth double that. I love art, I love it more than all my other property, they're so neat and compact, those rectangles of wealth.

But you have to win through to posterity, William, or you are worth nothing. You have to exist in the future, and for that you have to function in the present. I believe you have a yearning for an amendment to the Copyright Act. To apply it to the visual arts.

William . . . If I am to live.

Walpole See what I can do. Are you going home to Janey looking like that? – I'm not surprised she's bent.

Walpole gets back into his sedan chair and is carried off. William wraps the sheet tightly about him. He clutches at his head. Pause. The sedan chair returns. It is set down in front of him. Nothing happens.

William Was there something we forgot?

The chair opens and out steps Louisa. She is in tattered rags, and ravaged by an indescribably disgusting disease. The flesh hangs off her in strips. Her face is horribly disfigured. Her hands drip green slime.

Louisa Yes, Willy, we forgot about the pox, didn't we?

William (*in terror*) Louisa!

William tries to run but, as in a dream, his feet are like lead. Louisa reaches a slimy hand under his sheet and grabs his private parts.
Blackout.

SCENE SEVEN

An apartment in a palace. A large, ornate bed. A woman lies in it. Walpole, half-dressed, sits at a nearby table, writing. He screws up a sheet of paper and throws it away.

Walpole It's not as easy as I thought. The costume changes are a bugger. I need the heroine half-naked for the climax, so I've got to find a reason to get her off-stage and then I've got to find another reason to get her on-stage again. Give me the House of Commons any day. (*He looks to the woman.*) I know it won't be a popular law. But hang me a booming economy seems to breed subversion more than an age of hardship. It is precisely the popularity of the playhouses that renders them such a threat. Oh, I long to bring in a sensible, modern system, in which it is simply made plain to these chaps that it's in their own interests to toe the Lord Chamberlain's line . . . A hint here . . . A whisper there . . . Get the Artistic Director in for a cup of tea, wave a small cheque in his face . . . Just nudge the idea in. Where did the thinking spring from, that art must necessarily equal trouble? I am pacific, it is my nature, I believe with all my heart that what we need for the growth of the nation is peace. I don't like trouble and nor do the people. We like a quiet life and a decent dinner and why can't these toe-rags accept it? – Ah! Good! (*He writes fast.*) Get your costume off, you difficult old bag.

The woman in the bed is Queen Caroline.

Queen (*German accent*) I do not remember saying you could get up and work.

Walpole Oh, I thought we had done.

Queen Undress.

Walpole It's a critical scene!

Queen Undress!

Walpole Yes, your Majesty.

Queen We don't approve of censoring the people's entertainment. It's not the kind of thing we're used to in this country. It seems not to accord with our sense of what is England.

Walpole It won't be censorship, not outright censorship, I'd never get anyone to vote for that – just a system of licensing, a regulating hand on the temperamental shoulder. The actual dirty work of censoring will be done by the artists themselves. That's the beauty of it.

Queen So every play must get a licence. Then can they be performed?

Walpole But of course! If they can get a licence.

Queen Might I suggest, Minister, that this proposal of yours contains an element of – malice?

Walpole History's built on the lowest of motives.

Queen And every man has his price. I know your pet remarks. You are taking an unconscionably long time with your trousers. When we give a royal command we expect you to perform. Quick!

Walpole Yes, your Majesty. I'm hurrying up.

Queen I want to gaze upon your flesh, your flabby, blotchy flesh, your sinews, the slack pink muscle of government.

Walpole It is not something I normally shows to the world, ma'am.

Queen It is not elegant. Not beautiful. Not art.

Walpole I can go if the mood has left you –

Queen I fully intend to take my pleasure. To see the user used.

Walpole Caroline . . .

Queen What your political opponents are saying, of course, is that the time is ripe for expansion, we have the wealth, we have the resources, the army and the navy, we could thrust across the globe in the search for brand-new markets. Our merchant class has aspirations, Robin. There is a spirit of adventure in the land, I smell it. It hints that you are finished. Unless someone protects you.

Walpole Your Majesty's nostril is ever acute. But what about the King?

Queen I am the reign. Through my husband I exercise power. Let him march up and down with his soldiers. That leaves me free to concentrate on more important matters, such as the religious life of the state. As you may have observed, the people are morally lax. We need some tough new bishops.

Walpole Oh, we do, we do.

Queen I wish to appoint one. Robertson.

Walpole What!

Queen An excellent man. High church but with rationalist tendencies.

Walpole I know a better bet for a mitre – a chaplain who's demonstrated that the plays of our times offend against fourteen hundred texts in the Bible.

Queen Don't try to manipulate me. I have discussed the calculus with Leibnitz and astronomy with Newton. I am concerned with serious theology, not the sad boasts of the village idiot.

Walpole But Robertson will vote against me in the Lords! The balance of power will be upset!

Queen (*a smile*) Dear me. That sounds a terribly tenuous system. How will you get your Licensing Act through?

Walpole I'm working on a scheme, don't worry. (*He indicates his writing.*)

Queen But then you will need your Royal Assent.

Walpole . . . The price of which is a Bishop, is it? This is going to cost me a fortune in the long run. For that, will you also consider a little bit of business regarding the laws of copyright, which I beg leave to introduce?

Queen All I wish you to introduce at this moment, Prime Minister, is your tongue, your big, fat, talkative tongue.

Walpole It seems only fair and logical to me that, as we legislate to clarify the ownership of all our other products, so we should do the same for art.

Queen All right, all right! But why have you still your woollens on? Did I not say naked? Naked and kneeling before your Queen?

Walpole Majesty. (*Reluctantly he continues undressing.*)

Queen Wait. I have changed my mind.

He groans.

The carnal urge has suddenly left me. I think I'd sooner talk to the Archbishop. You may go.

Walpole starts to dress.

Go! At once! Audience over!

Walpole (*bowing*) Your humble servant, madam.

Humiliated, Walpole scoops up his clothing and his papers and bows his way out. Pause. Then the Queen collapses in a fit of hysterical laughter.

SCENE EIGHT

*A pillory. Still the same night. In the stocks stands Mrs
Needham. Egg, rotten fruit, and blood drip from her face.*

Mrs Needham God is good. (*Pause.*) God is just.
(*Pause.*) He is, he is! Prostitution is a wicked trade,
I knew he wouldn't like it. But this sinner will hang on
her cross, O merciful Father, until she hears your voice
call down from heaven in forgiveness, Needham, the
Bawd, you have suffered enough, pucker your lips on the
soles of my feet, we shall enter Jerusalem together. I wish
to announce my retirement from business. I have some
capital, Lord, not as much as I'd hoped for given my
talents – oh, I was a goer in my time, I could take ten
bob with my legs together – but that was when I free-
lanced. Once you become an employer your overheads
hit the roof . . . And the paperwork!

*Behind her, William comes on out of the dark. He still
wears only sheet and wig. He creeps on furtively,
shaking with cold.*

But if I survive the night, Christ Jesus, I will give my life
and my savings to your mission on earth. Let me be your
handmaiden, let me be your scourge in the city of sin.
For I know the guilty. I can name names. You will see
some blushing faces I promise you! – Who's there?

William's behind her. She can't turn round.

Who is it? Come where I can see you. I smell you! You
reek of gin.

William just stands there.

Don't hurt me, don't harm me, I haven't done anything
awful, but a mob of screaming puritans got hold of me

73

tonight, priests and thin women, I don't mind, allow them their outrage, there was a wave of morality burst upon us after Mr Walpole's constables had raided that theatre. And they dragged me to the Justice and he slammed me in the stocks! And then the apprentice boys pushed stones in their rotten tomatoes, and pelted me half to death! If you would wipe my face . . .? Be kind to me . . .? I'm cut in a thousand places . . . by the fruit of the self-righteous . . .

William puts a hand on her.

Oh! Mister! Your hand on my rump . . . I have the hindquarters of a horse, haven't I? I once heard of a gentleman who said England was a paradise for women, and hell for horses. Well he can take me out for a canter any old time. Little dig in the flanks and I'm off, mate. Oh, don't abuse me, don't, I feel so vulnerable, I'm dripping blood and egg-yolk, I can see it on the ground, like a little kiddie's painting of the sun.

William, from behind, pulls off the woman's skirt and puts it round himself.

Don't please! I'm dry! I'll scrape! A whore can be raped, you know, just as a bankrupt can be swindled. Lord Jesus protect me . . .

William pulls off her blouse and puts that on.

Do I know you? Is that it? Are you someone I have had? Some complainer out of all the happy thousands, bent on getting it for nothing? Will you speak to me, you pervert!

William tries on her shoes. They fit.

I will die of freezing . . . I'll be gone by dawn . . . But God will punish you. God will burn your lecher's eyes out. He will tear at your heart with his fingernails. God's fingernails, matey, think of that! God's rasping scratching omnipresent nails!

William, now dressed, drapes the sheet over the woman's head, and leaves.

Wanker! Pass by on the other side, then! Go on! Pass by! I can hear you shuffling away . . . Devil!

He is gone. Pause. Slowly her head droops.

Lord have mercy on me. Christ have mercy on me. Lord have mercy on me. Christ have mercy on me.

Fade out.

SCENE NINE

William's studio. Canvases stacked against the walls. Easels. Clutter. Enter Jane, with Sarah, who is holding a knife to her back. Sarah motions Jane to stay still. She herself wanders round looking at pictures with a great curiosity.

Sarah Has he ever painted you?

Jane No.

Sarah Why not? It's very odd. You'd think he'd want to paint his wife. Specially if she looked as clean and nice as you do.

Jane Oh, I'm very plain.

Sarah You're prettier than me.

Jane You have more character.

Sarah But no money to pay.

Jane Well, he had a commission to do you, didn't he?

Sarah Oh? Who from?

Jane How should I know? I don't keep up with all his business dealings.

Sarah I thought you said you handled the money . . .?

Pause. Sarah finds William's sword, hanging in its scabbard over the corner of a painting. She takes it out. She puts the knife aside. She examines the gleaming sword with pleasure.

You gone very quiet. I kill with delight, lady. That's what I'm like. It's how I make my mark. (*Pause.*) I thought, do one intelligent thing before I die. Get my future back. I was surprised I could be moved like that. I thought I was rock, a wall of granite, I thought I was the cliff that the waves bash against but never get inside of. But suddenly I was awash with it. Indignation. Well, shite, the cheek of it, to take my face and – ! (*Pause.*) Once you've made the big decision all the others make themselves. Long time since I've seen the smoky London streets. The fug whirled and eddied round me as I ran, my feet asplash in rivulets of piss, my neck and buttocks clenched expecting knife or fist or hammer. I came the back way. Through the shadows to Covent Garden. Now tell me truly why he's never painted you.

Jane . . . I don't want to be painted.

Sarah You do.

Jane I don't! Time and again I refuse him permission. I won't let him put me in that role, the role of the subject. I am not his subject, I am his lover and his wife, and I will never let him do my portrait, I will never surrender up that kind of power.

Sarah God, I wish I had your brain.

Jane You could have, I'll tutor you, I'll discover you to yourself, only put the sword away, Sarah, will you?

Sarah You been tutoring your husband, too, from what he says.

Jane Oh? What does he say?

Sarah He says you've got him thinking like a woman now. It all went over my head, rather.

Jane I simply want to make him think about his side of the bargain. The contract of marriage.

Sarah Why?

Jane Because I want it to last, I suppose.

Sarah Why?

Jane Because I love him. For all his faults. Heaven knows why I'm telling this to you. You want to murder him.

Sarah Whatever gave you that idea? (*Pause.*) How does he expect to put the whole of me, all my doings, all my dreams and disappointments in a few small dollops of paint? He done me in a prison in a city full of smoke. That's not me. That's not how I think of me. I think of me out in the open. Flat on my back in a hayrick, beneath a mackerel sky, dreaming of all the treats I'll have when I comes up to town . . . Ambition is a curse!

Jane It's not.

Sarah A fucking bane, ambition! A noose around your neck, that constant, constant yearning for more. Look at me for an example. Product of impossible desires.

Jane Oh, don't say that. Think of what William's achieved!

Sarah . . . Tell us yours then.

Sarah is leafing through bundles of drawings.

Jane It's not my place to have ambition. What could I do with it if I had it? I want my husband to get on. He is my voice, through him I make my presence felt. He is the one with the power. But I can tug him in certain directions, I can tweak his pencil as it skims across the paper. I've made him think a lot harder about the way he portrays women, for example. You find me there in the pictures, my brain in his brushstrokes . . .

Sarah I couldn't do it.

Jane Why, are you too proud?

Sarah No, I ain't proud.

Jane Yes, you are, I think.

Sarah I cut and slashed my pride. I butchered it. (*Pause.*) The difference is, that you believe in a time to come. Because you love. I don't. I don't know what it's like.

Jane It's a mixture . . . of being amazed and appalled by someone. Some of his tender sentiments amaze me. Whereas some of his habits in the toilet can be truly upsetting. It's a fine balance. If you're more amazed than appalled, you're probably in love. You're also in trouble, because you can be –

Sarah Used.

Jane Yes. Luckily William's too naive to sense when he might have me under his thumb.

Sarah I've got a feeling you ought to have a look at these.

Sarah shows Jane a series of drawings.

Jane Ugh, disgusting!

Sarah Mucky, yes.

Jane That's pornographic!

Sarah That's you.

Jane What?

Sarah That's you, that's a drawing of you. With a man's knob in your mouth.

Jane And another in –

Sarah He's got an imagination, hasn't he?

Jane Oh God!

Sarah He's done your portrait a hundred times.

Jane (*for the first time her composure cracks*) Oh my God! I'm going to be sick. – No I'm not, I'm going to kill him. Is that what he would like me to do? Look, there is pain on my face! My lover dreams of me degraded! Ugh! Look at that! And that! And that! Horrible, horrible man!

She tears up the drawings, ripping at them in fury, stamping on them, flinging them round the room. Sarah watches calmly. Jane eventually quietens down.

How sad his life must be.

SCENE TEN

William makes his way through London, dressed in skirt, blouse, high-heeled shoes and wig. From the shadows comes a low wolf-whistle. William stops, frightened. From another corner comes a man's laugh.
William picks up his skirts and runs.

SCENE ELEVEN

The studio. William enters.

William Made it. Christ what a night.

He gets a drink, sits in his favourite chair and shuts his eyes. Sarah emerges from hiding and stands in front of him, holding the sword. He sees her.

Oh, fuck! Don't you ever give up? And that's my sword! (*An explanation comes to him.*) I'm asleep. It's all right. (*He sits down again.*)

Sarah I broke out of prison.

William (*unimpressed*) Well done.

Sarah I come for my picture.

William Don't be a berk, I'm not handing over valuable pictures to a wisp of bleeding ectoplasm, am I.

Sarah pricks him with the sword.

Bitch! You're real! Christ!

Jane emerges from a hiding place.

Jane Yes, William, she is completely real.

William Jane!

Jane (*stares at him*) Why are you dressed like that?

William . . . I've suddenly gone very muzzy in the head, perhaps I better go and have a lie down.

Sarah (*sword*) Stay there!

William (*to Sarah*) You keep out of this, it's purely domestic, this. (*To Jane.*) It's a practical joke.

Jane You rotten lying pig!

William Please, please don't be difficult, darling, I've had such a terrible day.

Jane Why not? Why not be difficult?

Sarah Chop his knackers off.

William Oh, leave it out.

Jane Where have you been, then?

William I was with the lads, I ran into some of the lads, and I'd forgotten it was the first night of Harry's play, and they dragged me along and I admit we had one or two beers, I'm not perfect, I have my weak points and the booze is one of them, yes, anyway it was a huge success you ask anybody and we all ended up in the actresses' dressing-room, Harry insisted we all went backstage, because there was a – bit of a party, and I was prevailed upon to do a comic turn in female attire, that's another thing I've not told you about, but Jane we haven't been married that long, I'm renowned for this number I do in a frock, and then do you know what? The theatre was raided by Walpole's men and you don't believe a bloody word of this do you?

Sarah We found your drawings.

William Drawings, what drawings, the place is full of drawings – ?

Jane Drawings of me.

William I've never done a drawing of you, you don't allow it! (*Pause.*) Ah. Those drawings.

Jane Well? What have you got to say about them?

William . . . I think I got the proportions of your legs all wrong, but then I was working from –

Jane I hate you!

Sarah Chop his nuts off, I say.

William No!

Jane But those pictures, Will!

William I'm sorry!

Jane Of me in the sexual act!

William God, I'm sorry, I don't know what got into me, I'm very very sorry.

Jane Not good enough!

William Jane . . .!

Jane Not good enough! Not nearly! I devote my life to you. And how do you repay me? With ridicule and filth. I had somehow got this cranky notion that you were a sensitive man. But you're not, are you, you're just ordinary, this is what saddens me, you're just like all the rest!

William Who says? What bum-hole smears my honour?

Jane Sir Robert Walpole. Told us a tale. About a silver plate.

William Ah . . . well . . . Have faith in me, Janey, I may have done some daft things, but sweetheart, it's the same old Will under all his baggage.

Jane That's what I'm worried about. Whatever possessed you to do those awful drawings?

William Look, it's the pressure, that's what it is . . . I sit at my table and I fiddle with my charcoal and my mind is off and away, I don't even realise I'm doing it, there are nightmare things that I have got caged up, hairy, growling, they scrabble at the skin of me, and sometimes slither out. Have you noticed there is that quality of horror in even my gentlest work? How did it get there? What is there in me that I cannot seem to tame? I'm quite a nice bloke really! I'm only trying to make my way in the world. And I do it all for you. Everything, for you.

Jane (*softly*) You silly little fool, why do you always have to learn the hard way? Fail! For heaven's sake, fail! Be a disaster! Be a pauper! I wouldn't love you any the less.

They gaze into each others' eyes. Sarah, whose presence they have forgotten, slips the sword up under William's skirt. He stands on tiptoe.

Sarah (*quietly*) Listen, you pair of lovebirds, I want my pissing shitting picture back and by fuck I want it now.

William . . . I'm afraid I've got some rather bad news.

Sarah What?

William I ain't got it.

Jane Where is it?

William I dropped it off at the printer's.

Sarah We'll go and get it.

William He'll be closed.

Sarah We'll get the key.

William I don't know where he lives, I'm sorry!

Sarah Why did you take it to a printer's?

William Oh, I've got someone working on the plate.

Sarah What's the plate?

William To make the copies.

Sarah Copies . . .? One picture, I thought. One painting, to hang in a rich man's study, and stare down relentless with loathing and hate, a curse on every generation! But no, not good enough for Mr Up-to-the-minute, you'd have me printed on a thousand sheets of paper, clogging up the gutters, plugging cracks in tavern walls, eat and sleep and crapped on, by them that think they're good . . .? And I'll be on sale at me execution, will I, with me last words in print before I've said 'em?

William I am an artist. I exist to put the world in pictures.

Sarah Well you're not putting me. Come on, we're off to this printer's.

William We can't get in!

Sarah We'll kick down the door!

William One small problem. I never went to the printer's.

Jane You never went to the theatre, either, did you?

William No, I . . . We . . . We went to a gambling club.

Jane Oh, William!

William I gambled away my money, my clothes – and your picture.

Sarah Oh, shite! Who to?

William A man I didn't know – with a long hooked nose and a limp.

Sarah You are fucking lying, aren't you! Right!

William I think I'll be able to win it back tomorrow, I'm feeling very lucky!

Jane Don't hurt him, Sarah, please!

Sarah raises the sword to strike William. He dodges away. Jane tries to hold Sarah's arm. At that moment Louisa enters, with a crash.

William Lou! What do you want?

Louisa I changed my mind.

She throws his clothes down in the middle of the room.

Sarah Who are you?

Jane She's a common prostitute.

William – Who does a bit of laundry on the side!

Jane Is that where you've spent the evening? Up this woman's skirts?

William Wait! Give me a chance to think!

Sarah Why've you come here?

Louisa I was invited.

Jane No you weren't.

Louisa My turn, I thought, to paint a picture. A very private portrait. Of Willy and his ways.

William Oh, no.

Sarah What, has he done you too?

Louisa I can't be sure, I never seen them. – You robbing him, are you?

Sarah No, he's robbing me.

Louisa Up and up he goes. I watch from in the gutter. Daubing paint on canvas with his fingers like a kid smearing shit on walls. And they buy it! They pay money for it! In the salons and soirées of the West End, they dip into the hot-pot of his brains, and what do they find? Pictures of a prostitute. Dying of the clap.

Jane He's just a man. You have to make allowances.

Louisa Fine, in that case I can tell you how he likes to lie down on the floor and have me stand over him heaving and straining and –

Jane Stop it! Stop it! Why are you doing this?

Louisa Because I loved him. Once.

Jane (*shock*) You? Why?

Louisa Well – why do you?

William (*glum*) Why does anybody?

Sarah Belt up.

Jane Be quiet.

Louisa Shut your fucking trap.

William With a bit of luck I'm imagining all this.

Louisa But can you distinguish any more? Between pencil lines and people? You pin us like moths to your paper and you sit and watch us squirm.

Sarah That's right, he does, that's right.

Louisa I'm finished, Will. I'm all wore out. Unsellable. Just wanted you to see.

Sarah I know how you feel. He done one of me and all.

Jane (*to Louisa*) Please go. I think you've said enough.

Sarah Fucking shut up, you, we're talking about art.

Louisa (*to Jane*) How can you stick with him? Despite everything you know?

Jane He is my husband. He loves me.

Louisa What makes you think he won't betray you? To get another step up that bleeding ladder he's got lodged in his head?

Sarah (*to Louisa*) Tell me how he done you, the composition and that.

Louisa (*to Jane*) We drag ourselves down, do you know that, not him, not anyone, *us*. Love? I shit on love. Daily.

Sarah (*urgent*) Tell me how he done you!

Louisa (*weary*) What difference does it make?

Sarah He sat me at a table. In a beam of light from the window. The shadows falling on the filth and straw. He were going to put my gaoler in but then he said he wouldn't. Good job too 'cause I've killed him. (*Laughs.*) Wouldn't look too bright, would it? Picture of me in a prison cell I've just escaped from being guarded by a bloke I've just done up.

Louisa Oh my God . . . You're Sarah Sprackling, are you?

Sarah That's right.

Louisa Then – this is meant to be you?

Louisa produces the sketch of Sarah and unrolls it.

Sarah Me picture!

Louisa I've been staring and staring, thinking . . . how does she feel?

Sarah Give it!

William No!

Sarah I said give it!

William Don't, Lou, please!

Jane Look out!

Sarah lunges for the picture and spears it on the point of her sword.

Sarah Now I have you, I have you at last. My little darling. Now I have a hold of you. Tried to go off on your own, din't you? Tried to give me the slip. (*She holds the paper to a candle flame.*) Oh, doesn't that look pretty. That pretty blushing face. Burn you whore! And don't never desert me again.

The picture burns.

I got this fantastical feeling running up and down my backbone like a ball of lightning, whoosh. Quiver of sleeping flesh come suddenly to life. I set out to do a thing and I done it. What a fucking wonderful feeling.

The picture is gone. She lays down the sword.

All done now.

Jane Then please – go.

Sarah Yes. Be dawn soon. Be time soon.

Louisa What way are you walking?

Sarah East. Back to Newgate.

Louisa To the hangman?

Sarah Coming with me? Keep me company?

Louisa Why don't you run for it? Go on, run for it, run free, take off across Islington Fields and vanish . . . Sleep by day and run by night . . . Change your identity, become someone else . . .

Sarah I am just barely smart enough to be me, what chance have I got of becoming someone else?

Louisa But surely you don't want to die?

Sarah Yes, I do. Who wants to live like this?

Louisa I'm confused, I don't understand – why?

Sarah . . . Tooth of a hanged person supposed to be a love potion, ain't it. Some unloved woman will pluck my yellow stumps. Grind them in some farmboy's porridge. And I hope she gets some pleasure from it, too. Little snatch of warmth in the cold time, just now, aching for the sun after the chaos of the night . . . Will you do me a favour?

Louisa I might. What?

Sarah Come along the road and I'll tell you.

They go off together. William grabs a piece of paper and a pencil and begins to sketch fast.

Jane Thank God they've gone . . . Trembling like a leaf . . . What are you doing?

William Ssh! Sketching from memory, technical memory, got to concentrate –

Jane I beg your pardon?

William Get it down the printer's first thing in the morning.

Jane William! No! (*Snatches away his pencil.*) Let the poor woman die gracefully.

William Gracefully? You call that gracefully?

Jane She thinks it is.

William She's bonkers!

Jane William, I have to say it, I think this is immoral.

William I know that. I'm not thick.

Jane Think how she'd feel if you published her picture now!

William Christ, she'll never know!

Jane She is choosing when to die. What else has she ever chosen in her life? Perhaps that has a kind of grace. (*Pause.*) Abandon it. For me.

William (*concedes*) The world will never hear of Sarah Sprackling, she will never have existed, she will be a ghost, who stalks the landscape of my brain, how's that?

Jane Thank you. I am going back to bed now. We shall discuss all this tomorrow. (*Pause.*) The thought of you with that old whore . . .! Ugh! And Robert Walpole. You're in too deep! And oh, when I saw those vile drawings, I was livid! But then I stopped and calmed down and tried to think sensibly about it and – I began to look on you as, well, what shall we say? Cripple? Some sort of emotional cripple? Not got the use of all your bits. And all I can feel for one of those is pity. Goodnight. (*Exits.*)

William Night night, sweetheart.

Immediately, from another entrance, a Stage-hand enters, crosses the stage, gives William a camera, and exits.

Oh. Thanks.

William examines the camera with great interest. Immediately Jane returns. William guiltily hides the camera behind his back.

Jane And don't have any more to drink tonight, William, or you will ruin your health. (*Exits.*)

Immediately Oliver appears from another entrance, looking thoroughly debauched. He advances on

William from behind, seeing only the costume. He
grabs at William's bum.

Oliver My dear! I came.

William (*turns*) Oliver!

Oliver Oh, bother, it's you, is it? I thought I'd find Janey
here alone.

William What?

Oliver I will not be hobbled by convention, it's so very
dreary, don't you think? I spend my nights up a lot of
loose streetgirls, but it's no good, I don't come off. I need
a female of good breeding. Your wife will do. Is that all
right?

William Er . . .

Oliver One has to do what gives one pleasure, William.
The world may end tomorrow. Pop. Then what are you
left with?

William That's not a bad argument. Here, do you know
how to work one of these?

Oliver Yes, you look in here, push this, and –

A flash. Oliver takes a photo of William. William
takes the camera back and stares at the photograph.

William That's amazing.

Jane enters, seductively dressed.
She embraces Oliver, and leads him aside. They
make love. She calls out to her husband.

Jane William. William.

William sees them now, and starts to take photographs
of them. Harry enters.

Harry Hello, Will.

William Wotcher, Harry.

*Harry kisses William passionately on the mouth.
William is surprised, but doesn't resist. Walpole
enters.*

Walpole (*stern*) William . . .

William I'm a bit involved at the moment. With my
friend.

*Walpole produces a knife and sticks it in Harry's
back. Harry dies.
   William jumps away.*

Now look what you've done!

Walpole It's all right, I'll get away with it.

*Walpole goes towards Oliver and Jane. Harry sits up.
William yelps. Walpole turns. Harry blows a raspberry
at Walpole. Walpole blows a bigger raspberry at Harry.
Walpole goes to Jane and joins in. Frank enters with a
mouthful of money. He spits the money at William.*

Frank My turn.

Frank goes to Jane and joins in.

Harry And mine.

*Harry goes to Jane and joins in. William photographs
the proceedings.*

William Christ, this is good. Jane, I'm disgusted with
you. What a slut. I'm appalled! Four at once! Bloody
hell. – Here, lift your leg a fraction.

*We see photographs everywhere. Jane jumps up, runs
back and points at William.*

Jane Now! Get him! Get him good!

*The Drummer enters, playing a pounding beat. Jane
exits. The four men advance on William.*

William Oh no . . .

*They chase him and strip him of his clothes. He tries
to scrabble away but he is surrounded. The drumbeat
drives into his brain. Each of the men produces a
camera, all with flash.*

Walpole Now! Take his picture! Take his picture! Put
him in the file! Put him in the file!

*They all photograph a naked and terrified man
crouching on the floor.*

William Jane! Janey! Janey! Janey! Janey! Jan-ey!

*Jane enters, now restored to her normal demure self,
and dressed once again in her nightclothes, yawning.
Immediately all the dream figures exit. All Jane can
see is the sobbing William.*

Jane Oh, Will . . . oh, darling. (*Takes him in her arms.*)

William Janey, it was nasty, it was you, you were doing
it with Oliver and you were – nasty pictures –

Jane Now come along. I don't think you're very well,
are you, darling?

She wraps him in a blanket and leads him to bed.

It's dawn. Come along with me to bed. Little boy needs a
proper rest. Let's get you tucked up.

She puts him into bed. He sobs.

It's all right, cry. Cry and cry. You can't keep it all
rammed down inside. You have to let people know of
your feelings for them. It's vital, Will, it really is.

Otherwise your work is a lie. Isn't it? (*Pause. She looks out of the window.*) It's starting to snow. Winter. – I'll let you paint me if you want. Do you want? I'd sooner we had it all out in the open. Paint me, I can contain it. Knowing what I know. I will not let go of you, for the sake of a little pride. (*Laughs gently.*) You and your silly dreams. Oliver and I indeed! He is such a dreadful rake. (*Pause.*) Snow covering up everything now. All the birds will fly away. Where do they go, Will? Some unmapped land? Can you see it in your head? (*She gets into bed.*) I will guard you. I will guard your reputation. Sleep now. Deep down underground like a tulip bulb. Sleep now, and come up later.

> *She lies down and pulls the covers over their heads. Immediately Sarah drops from above, dangling on the end of a rope. She swings at the foot of the bed. Louisa runs on, grabs Sarah's legs, and pulls downwards with all her weight. Sound of the crowd roaring at the hanging. Spot on Louisa, her eyes wide with horror, and fade.*

SCENE TWELVE

Several months later, by the banks of the Thames. Low tide at a 'stairs' or landing-place at Wapping. Steps leading down from the wharf to the river. Ancient wooden beams and posts. An old boat overturned on the mudbank. Harry stands on the steps. He writes on a scrap of paper. He stops writing. He is dejected. Frank and Oliver enter above, along the wharf. Oliver has the black patches on his neck and face which signify a pox. The scene starts slow and quiet.

Frank The ice is breaking up.

Pause.

Oliver I hate spring.

Pause.

Frank We need a boat to ferry us downriver.

Oliver I hate sunshine. I hate it when the daffodils come out.

Pause.

Frank There's Harry.

Harry (*turns*) It's happened. Walpole's closed me down.

Frank Yes, we passed the Act last night, late night sitting you know.

Oliver You didn't vote for it, did you?

Frank I gave my maiden speech, against the motion.

Oliver Brave man.

Frank Then I voted for it.

Oliver Quite. So did I in the Upper House.

Harry I now have to apply to the office of the Lord Chamberlain for a licence to perform any new interlude, tragedy, comedy, opera, play, farce, prologue or epilogue. Or I shall be deemed a rogue and a vagabond and punished accordingly.

Oliver That is what you wanted, is it not?

Harry But how am I supposed to make a living?

Frank Get along and apply for the blessed licence. We all have to abide by the law.

William enters, looking affluent in a new coat.

Oliver The genius himself has come along. This is indeed an honour.

William Hullo, lads. Aren't I just a Beefsteak like the rest of you?

Frank Long time since we've seen you at a meeting.

William . . . And where are we going today?

Oliver Down the Thames to Kent. (*With distaste.*) The green fields of Kent.

Frank We have undertaken to provide the aesthetic education of an English artist. This will be your Grand Tour. The fruity air of Kent will lend you inspiration.

William What for?

Harry The art of the dung-heap.

William . . . Thought you were a bit quiet.

Harry I've seen your advertisements. In the press.

Oliver Oh, yes, bravo! Astonishment in the coffee-shops! The general view is, with this new Copyright Act, you'll become the first English painter to succeed without patronage.

Harry 'The Rake's Progress'.

William Yes?

Harry 'The Rake's Progress'.

William You don't like the title.

Harry It's just sex. You're obsessed with sex.

William Am I fuck. It's a serious work. Me and Jane spent the whole winter on it. What I'm obsessed with is beauty. The truth about beauty.

Harry There is no truth about beauty. Beauty disguises truth. It is impossible to write a beautiful play.

Frank Ignore him, Will. The Prime Minister's just shut his theatre.

Oliver He read out a play in Parliament. It's called *The Golden Rump*.

Frank It's filthy. Mr Walpole says he got if off a theatre manager, who hinted Henry Fielding was the author.

Harry Which is quite impossible, I couldn't plot a play that amateurishly if I tried.

Beat.

Oliver There's a boat.

Frank Hey, Waterman! – There's some old biddy in it.

They go down towards the river.

William You coming?

Harry No. I've no business in Kent. I've met a very nice girl, I think I'd sooner be with her.

William Look, what's the matter with you?

Harry Nothing, absolutely nothing.

William You have to try, Harry. You have to make an effort.

Harry Why?

William God, what is the world coming to, when you can't even talk to your mates.

Harry You've done a deal, haven't you? They're calling it Hogarth's Act, do you know that? What do you have to do, Will, to get your name on the statute books? What do you have to sell?

William Well if you're going to be like that you can stick it up your arse.

William goes to Frank and Oliver.

Harry Oh, fuck . . .

William Harry ain't coming.

Oliver Oh, leave him to sulk.

William That our boat?

William exits to the river.

Harry Will, we're supposed to be friends, everyone thinks we're friends . . .!

But he's gone. Mrs Needham enters from the river. She wears black, and carries a crucifix and a bible.

Frank Welcome to London, madam. Christ alive, it's her.

Oliver Mrs Needham. Bonjour.

Mrs Needham Good morning, boys. Off to church?

Frank We are going on a peregrination.

Mrs Needham I see. Was that Mr Hogarth I just passed, whose 'Harlot's Progress' has turned so many maidens off the downward path to hell?

Frank Yes.

Mrs Needham Thought so. Here, boatman, here's a ha'penny tip.

She lobs a coin towards the boat. But she throws badly and it falls into the mud below. She gives Frank another coin.

Oh, silly me, Lord forgive my wastefulness. My spell in the stocks, it withered my arms. Please, Frank, give the man this and tell him I will pray for his safety upon the foaming waters. Is there any act of sacrifice I can perform for either of you? Any good deed? No? (*Low voice.*) I've got a pair of twins.

Oliver Twins?

Mrs Needham Yes.

Oliver Identical?

Mrs Needham Here and there. Like to try, Viscount?

Oliver Twins! I've never had twins before.

Frank Oliver, come on.

Oliver Perhaps when I get back . . .

Frank Cast off, Will!

Exit Frank and Oliver. Mrs Needham goes up the steps to Harry.

Mrs Needham Young fellow? We're back to business as usual. Except on Sundays, I don't hold with trading on the Sabbath.

Harry shakes his head. Mrs Needham shrugs and exits. Harry sobs. A figure emerges from under the upturned boat. It is Louisa. She is utterly filthy and decrepit. She slithers across the mud, making for the coin dropped by Mrs Needham.

Harry My God.

Louisa (*gets the coin*) What do you want?

Harry Do you live under there?

Louisa Gives shelter from the wind, doesn't it?

Harry But how do you survive?

Louisa The wind blows particles of clever stuff all round me.

99

Harry I see. Are you alone?

Louisa Yes.

Harry What's it like?

Louisa It's sad.

Harry I'm sad too.

Louisa Don't come near me, I got a disease!

Harry Can I help?

Louisa No one can help. It just blows and blows and blows. And blows and blows and blows and blows and blows.

Harry I run a theatre. And I write the plays. They've just closed it down. That's why I'm sad.

Louisa My my. Dear dear. What a pity. – Look! (*She leaps across the mud.*) Lugworm! (*She scrabbles with her hands.*) Gone. Bugger! Not quick enough.

Harry I'm not allowed to work!

Louisa Very juicy, lugworms. I like a lugworm as a starter.

Harry What am I going to do? To hang on to my dignity?

Louisa I haven't got the faintest idea. I'm far too busy to go to the theatre. – Look! Out on the river! Oh look!

Harry Oh yes!

> *From the direction of the river, the sound of Handel's 'Water Music'. Coloured lights play on the mudbank as a boat glides slowly past. The sound of voices comes indistinctly from midstream.*

I've never seen it before. And it is – despite everything, isn't it – amazingly beautiful . . .

Louisa Yes! Yes! – What is it?

Harry Why, it's the royal barge! And that one coming along behind is the barge for the musicians, do you see? That's an orchestra! Floating down the middle of the river! And look – there on the foredeck – that's the Queen!

Louisa The Queen?

Harry Yes, and there's bloody Walpole talking to her, kissing her hand! Oh, the bastard! You're an arsehole, Walpole! You're a shit!

Louisa Will you be quiet! That's the Queen, for goodness' sake! She doesn't want to hear that kind of language! (*She goes down on her knees in the mud.*) The Queen of England. All my life I've wanted to see the Queen, and now I have, it is complete. On my river! In front of my eyes! Your Majesty! Your Majesty!

Harry You're right. What point in yelling? Must find another way. Some system harder to control.

Louisa It's a royal wedding, is it? Oh, I love a wedding! I love to see the happy bride! These people, they're so pretty, so clever! And the colours! And the music! And the flags!

Harry I'm thinking of writing a novel.

Louisa A what? What's one of them?

Harry Hard to explain. They're new.

Blast of 'Water Music'. Slow fade on Harry and Louisa. The lights of the Royal Barge. The sounds of a party: laughter, conversation, glasses being smashed.

Blackout.

THE TASTE OF THE TOWN

a companion play to
The Art of Success

The Taste of the Town was first performed at Rose Theatre Kingston, in repertoire with *The Art of Success*, on 21 September 2018. The cast, in alphabetical order, was as follows:

William Hogarth Keith Allen
Nancy/Mrs Ryott Ruby Bentall
Mrs Colquhoun/Mrs Bascombe Emma Cunniffe
Zachariah Blunt Ben Deery
Parson Venables Jack Derges
Samuel Bryan Dick
Horace Walpole Ian Hallard
Jane Hogarth Susannah Harker
Bridget Jasmine Jones
Lady Thornhill Sylvestra Le Touzel
David Garrick Mark Umbers

Director Anthony Banks
Set and Costume Designer Andrew D. Edwards
Video and Projection Designer Douglas O'Connell
Lighting Designer James Whiteside
Music Olly Fox
Sound Designer Max Pappenheim
Casting Director Stuart Burt
Fight Directors Rachel Bown Williams and
    Ruth Cooper Brown of RC-Annie Ltd
Assistant Director Ally Manson

Characters

William Hogarth
Jane Hogarth
Lady Thornhill
Bridget
Samuel
David Garrick
Zachariah Blunt
Mrs Colquhoun
Mrs Ryott
Horace Walpole
Mrs Bascombe
Boatman
Nancy
Parson Venables

Act One

SCENE ONE

Chiswick, a village outside London. It is roughly thirty years after The Art of Success.

The garden of William Hogarth's country retreat. It is dominated by a mulberry tree that is already old. At one side is the house; at the other is the painting room. There is a bench and a table. It's a glorious summer's morning.

Lady Thornhill, seventies, enters from the garden. She has a parasol. She sits on the bench. She feels her side; she has a pain. She looks up as Bridget, an Irish maid, enters from the painting room, carrying a tray with coffee things.

Lady Thornhill Good morning, Bridget.

Bridget Morning, My Lady. Isn't it a grand day?

Lady Thornhill It is warm. What's that you've got?

Bridget Coffee. Mrs Hogarth sent it out. Mr Hogarth didn't want it.

Lady Thornhill Why not?

Bridget I think 'tis the dog. His fondness for that animal!

Lady Thornhill Indeed. But in the end, Bridget, a dog is a dog. Where is your mistress now?

Bridget In the kitchen, with Cook.

Lady Thornhill Bid her come out, if you please.

Bridget Yes, My Lady.

Lady Thornhill Bridget? Is that still hot? I'll drink it.

Bridget turns back and sets out the coffee service on the table. Then she pours a cup of coffee.

Bridget Cream or milk, My Lady?

Lady Thornhill Oh, cream, cream.

Bridget pours cream, then bobs and goes indoors with the tray.
Lady Thornhill sips her coffee, but it tastes foul. She is pale and perspiring. She fans herself.
Jane Hogarth, about fifty, enters from the house.

Jane Mother – are you quite well?

Lady Thornhill I don't believe I am, dear. It's very warm today.

Jane Your hands are cold.

Lady Thornhill And there's something wrong with that coffee.

Jane tries the coffee.

Jane No, there isn't.

Lady Thornhill Then there's something wrong with me. Everything tastes like metal.

Jane Metal?

Lady Thornhill Yes, like I've been licking the fire-irons. Or biting the spoons.

Jane Have you?

Lady Thornhill Do I look like a person who eats her own cutlery? Though the flesh may be weak, my mind is unimpaired. But I suffer a pain in my – down here – a prodding pain, a provoker.

Jane Why haven't you mentioned this?

Lady Thornhill Oh, I don't want to be a burden.

Jane But you must tell me if you're ill!

Lady Thornhill I'm just an old woman, I know I'm not important.

Jane I'll send for a doctor.

Lady Thornhill No, don't. It will pass. It passes! No doctor! – Just sit with me for a minute. That's all I ask. Sit down.

With some reluctance, Jane sits. Lady Thornhill brightens up.

Jane Where's William?

Lady Thornhill In his painting room, with the drapes drawn. Pray tell me why he lives in the dark?

Jane He's fretting about the new picture.

Lady Thornhill Then the man's a fool. He's painted awful pictures before, and I've no doubt he'll paint awful pictures again. My husband never sat around moping, just because a picture didn't work.

Jane My husband is not your husband.

Lady Thornhill No, he is not, is he? Where is his 'Dome of Saint Paul's'? Where are his 'Sabine Women'? The best Master Hogarth can put his name to is a middling altarpiece in Bristol, which may only be viewed by squinting round a pillar. One has never seen a Resurrection look quite so unusual. A true artist, like your father, embraces scenes from history, mythology, scripture – not jades and hussies, squibs and satires. Oh but I forget! William has his 'Sigismunda'. Yes, he does have that. There is his grand style, his stab at the Sublime. Bah. Joshua Reynolds must be snorting in his soup!

Jane Please, don't mention Reynolds.

Lady Thornhill Painting is a contest. You know it, I know it. It's a fight. Reynolds is a bare-knuckle fellow, and your man isn't even in training.

Jane Are you feeling better, Mother?

Lady Thornhill I feel tip-top, thank you, Jane. There is nothing so reviving as a pleasant conversation. I am stuck out here alone, you know, miles from town –

Jane Six miles.

Lady Thornhill – miles from society, miles from everything, with not a soul to talk to but the maids, and nothing to distract me but a pain, a wretched, disagreeable pain which you seem to have entirely forgotten about.

Jane Oh, for pity's sake! Now you are being unreasonable!

Lady Thornhill Pray do not rebuke me. If I die this afternoon, you will regret it.

Jane You're not going to die this afternoon.

Lady Thornhill I think that's in the hands of the Almighty, don't you? When I am called, I shall go. Why are you so touchy, Jane dear? Has good humour gone out of fashion?

Jane I'm sorry. But can't you see how dispiriting it is, to have to look after everybody, all at once?

Lady Thornhill You have no children. Your time is your own.

Jane Ah. Yes, of course. I forgot about my carefree existence. If there is anything I can do to make you happy, Mother, I will do it, and gladly.

Lady Thornhill Will you, dear? Then take me shopping. Let's go shopping, at once!

Jane Could it not be tomorrow?

Lady Thornhill Tomorrow may be too late. Let's go to town! You promised!

Jane (*resigned*) Very well. We'll go, once Samuel returns with the carriage. – Yes, Bridget?

Bridget enters and approaches Jane. She has a calling card on a silver tray.

Bridget A gentleman to see you, ma'am.

Jane reads the card. She is pleased and excited.

Jane Oh! – Bring him through.

Bridget exits. Lady Thornhill takes the card and reads it.

Lady Thornhill Oh! How delightful!

The ladies arrange themselves to their best advantage. Bridget enters bringing David Garrick, early forties, the most famous actor of the century. He is in a beautiful riding outfit.

Bridget Mr Garrick, ma'am.

Jane Davy!

David bows graciously. Bridget exits to the house.

David My dear Lady Thornhill, it has been too long since we have seen you at Drury Lane. Why, the country air agrees with you! You look, dare I say, like a girl of nineteen, like a rose in the first rush of spring.

Lady Thornhill Do not flatter me.

David Ma'am, I would not dare.

Lady Thornhill (*happily*) I must believe you, then.

Jane What am I, Davy? A ragwort? A nettle?

David You know you can't compete with your mother.

Jane But were I a weed I could strangle her.

David My dear, true Jane, your light shines from within: you are the hidden gem of Chiswick.

Jane I could do with a polish, I think. And my setting has worked loose.

Lady Thornhill Please refrain from your metaphors, they are modish I know, but I find them tremendously tiresome.

Jane Will you take coffee?

David No, no, I am riding down to the villa. I shan't stay long.

Jane And Mrs Garrick? Is she well?

David Eva is well. She remains in town.

Lady Thornhill How is town?

David Town, Lady Thornhill, is a cauldron of envy, greed and malevolent gossip.

Lady Thornhill Oh, how lovely.

David Chiswick is very much pleasanter.

Lady Thornhill But what is the talk? What is the verdict on the new King?

David It's good. Apparently he can speak English.

Jane No!

Lady Thornhill A King who speaks English? How unusual.

David And he enjoys the theatre. The box office is humming – our best advance for years.

Jane You must be so busy! Why have you stopped to see us?

David Oh, Jane. Jane, Jane. I wish that were all the news. But a baleful rumour has reached my ears – a canard I am sure! – that the whole world is laughing at William.

Jane Laughing? Why? What has he done?

David He has done a new picture. And they say it does not suit.

Jane Which new picture?

David His most recent, I think.

Jane Not the 'Sigismunda'?

David Yes, that's it.

Jane But that's here, in the studio. It didn't sell.

David Jane, he has shown it to the public.

Jane No, he hasn't.

David Yes. At the new Exhibition, in town.

Jane Oh, God! Has he? Why?

Lady Thornhill Because he's soft in the head.

Jane Mama!

David He might need cheering up, I thought. Gossip can be hurtful; and these are people who have always praised him heretofore. God's hooks, but they are fickle!

Lady Thornhill Have you seen the 'Sigismunda', sir?

David I? No. Been in rehearsal. Rather intense.

Lady Thornhill Perhaps they are not fickle. Perhaps they have good taste.

Jane Should we not prepare for our outing?

Lady Thornhill (*to David*) Pray tell me sincerely: do you think he is a great painter? The wits at the clubs call him a sign-writer, and no more. In his own mind, he is the equal of Raphael, of Titian. Or even of Van Dyke! What is your opinion, Mr Garrick?

David He did Eva and me most prettily.

Lady Thornhill And her hands really look like that, do they? Like the overhanging branches of a tree?

David I own it, Lady Thornhill, a charming portrait of myself and my radiant wife. It shows her as a woman of wit and intelligence – my equal, almost – a blue-stocking, one might say! In short, it is a very modern picture, which I am proud to hang on my wall.

Lady Thornhill Mr Garrick. I was not displeased to see your Richard Crookback, nor your Lear. At both tragedy and farce you have no rival. You are the finest player upon the English stage. But you know nothing at all about art. (*Calls.*) Bridget! – I will bid you good day.

David (*bows*) Your Ladyship.

Jane I shan't be long, Mother.

Bridget enters.

Lady Thornhill She has upon her one of her dark moods, Mr Garrick. Beware. (*To Bridget.*) Help me dress for town.

Bridget Yes, My Lady.

Lady Thornhill Town! At last!

Lady Thornhill and Bridget exit to the house. Lady Thornhill leaves her parasol on the bench.

David How are his spirits?

Jane Very low. He doesn't eat, he doesn't sleep.

David Is he drinking?

Jane Goodness, no – he hasn't had a drink for years. But he is in a sort of deadly lethargy. He barely speaks to me.

David How on earth has this happened?

Jane Are you familiar with 'The Lady's Last Stake'? The picture he made for Lord Charlemont?

David Oh yes, oh my! The card game. Most amusing. The lady must decide whether to gamble her honour, which is all she has left. And here is her opponent, looking cocky. And here's little madam, about to accept the bet. (*He mimes it.*) And one just knows she's going to lose! And then he's going to give her a – (*He stops.*) I saw it in your house at Leicester Fields.

Jane So did Sir Richard Grosvenor, who commissioned Will to paint another, on any subject he chose, and to set his own price.

David He told William Hogarth to set his own price? Is the man an idiot?

Jane He is rich. Too rich. His family built Grosvenor Square. If only William had painted him a pretty girl with a saucy smile. But no. 'Sigismunda'.

David It is something from Dryden, I believe?

Jane Dryden had it from Boccaccio. The Princess Sigismunda is in love with a page-boy, Guiscardo. She marries him in secret. Her father finds out, has Guiscardo killed, and sends his heart to Sigismunda in a chalice. William has done the woman holding her dead lover's heart, about to drink poison and die. Sir Richard Grosvenor cordially detests it, and refuses to pay Will's price.

David Which is –?

Jane Four hundred and four pounds, five shillings.

David Four hundred pounds! But Jane, you could buy every canvas at the Exhibition for that sum! What was he thinking of?

Jane He was thinking of an Old Master – a Correggio, I believe – also a 'Sigismunda', which sold at auction last year for –

David Four hundred and four pounds, five shillings?

Jane Will insists that his is just as good.

David I'd better talk to him. Where is he?

Jane In the painting room, with the curtains drawn. Oh, goodness. What is to be?

David Jane, Jane. I run a company of actors, I'm familiar with this kind of thing – sitting in the dark, demanding money. It takes but a firm slap, a quick kiss, and the promise of a lead next season, and everyone is once again content. Leave it to me.

Bridget enters.

Bridget Lady Thornhill says please to help her choose her bonnet, ma'am.

Jane I'd better go in. Bridget, will you take Mr Garrick to the painting room? (*To David.*) Good luck.

David May I kiss your hand? The hand of an angel.

Jane I think I am fallen.

David Jane?

Jane I cannot be angelic all the time.

David No one can, not even me. Is it really that bad?

Jane It's awful! He was different, thirty years ago. Dynamic, and dangerous, and fun. Now it's as if the light has gone out. We shuffle around in the darkness.

David All will be well.

He reassures her, and Jane exits.

Your master painted your portrait, didn't he, Bridget? With the coachman, and the kitchen maids?

Bridget Sir, he did.

David Odd thing to do, don't you think? Paint the servants? Who does that?

Bridget He's a fair man, honest to God.

David cups her chin in his hand.

David You've a good profile. Are you from Dublin? I am much admired at Smock Alley in that city.

Bridget The single time I clapped eyes on Dublin was when I took the packet boat for here.

David You have a fine figure, too.

Bridget Thank you, I'm sure. Now, may I show you the way to –

David Stand still, girl.

Bridget does as she is told. David surveys her body.

Have you ever thought of going on the stage?

William Hogarth, sixty-three, enters from the painting room, blinking in the light. He is prosperous, a man of means; but here he wears a long dressing gown and a cap, with no wig. David reaches to touch Bridget's curves as William enters.

William Oi. Dave.

David (*all smiles*) Why, there you are! Good day to you!

William Bridget, I don't pay you to muck about. Get indoors.

Bridget exits quickly.

What are you up to?

David I had her in mind for a Juliet.

William Oh, is that what you call it? Behave.

Shaking his head, William turns back to the painting room.

David Will! Come back! You can't sit inside in the dark!

William I'm Serjeant-Painter to the bleeding King, I can sit where I want.

David I have come some distance to see you!

William Well, you can fuck some distance off again.

David Wait, wait! I dare not imagine quite how you are feeling. Life can be harsh, can't it?

William Yes.

David What can I do to help?

William You can fuck off home.

David Describe to me your emotions at this point.

William Oh, Christ.

David Will, Will, I am trying, merely, to be your friend. Open your heart, let us talk as brothers. Please.

William sits, despondent.

William I'm lost without him. Utterly lost.

David Lost without whom?

William That little dog.

David What little dog?

William Trump.

David Trump?

William My only friend.

David Will, you have many, many friends.

William None like him. That you can rely on. None like Trump.

David What's happened to Trump?

William He's fucking died, hasn't he? I get up one morning and he's fucking dead. Christ, what am I going to do?

David Is this all because of a dog?

William Why, what did you think it was all because of?

David I heard about a problem with a painting –?

William Have you got a dog?

David No, I haven't.

William Why not?

David Too busy. Eva has a spaniel. A King Charles.

William Eva would have a spaniel. Christ, I can just see Eva with a spaniel in her lap. What painting?

David I think you know.

William . . . You put in years and years of effort. Just so some arsehole can spit in your face.

David To whom are you referring?

William Well, my mother-in-law, for one.

David I am disinclined to believe Lady Thornhill has trained her arsehole in that way.

William You'd be surprised. She loathes my work. She thinks the name of her poor dead husband is going to ring down the ages, just because he done a few apostles. And my name will never mean nothing.

David Hogy, Lady Thornhill is your chiefest supporter. I was talking to her just now. She praised you in the highest degree.

William I don't know how you keep a straight face when you say that. She can't fucking stand the sight of me.

David No, she is old-fashioned, merely. She admires the Continental style.

William What's wrong with British style?

David There isn't one.

William There is!

David Not according to the connoisseurs. As far as I can see, the world of art is based on snobbery. Thank goodness it's not like that in the theatre.

William Look, I am not the dunce they take me for. I revere the great masters of paint. But the tossers that purchase their pictures? How can I reverence them? I don't see why, to be accorded any good, you're meant to churn out Crucifixions and Virgins and Saint Jeromes one after the other –

David You could do Saint Jerome –

William – with his bleeding lion.

David You could do a lion –

William No, David, I can't do lions! That's the point! My lions look like sheep! And my sheep look like dogs!

David What do your dogs look like?

William Me!

David I was going to suggest we go out for a walk.

William I am not going out for a walk.

David It's a lovely day. The sun is shining, the birds are singing –

William Bollocks.

He turns to go.

David Will! I thought you were a fighter! Where's your heart of oak? Your fists like battering-rams? Face your attackers boldly, armoured *cap à pied*. We all have enemies, you know!

William You haven't.

David No, that's true. Perhaps because I try to please my public? They love me because I give them what they want: great acting; nice frocks; the masterpieces of Shakespeare, Congreve, Jonson –

William Suitably rewritten –

David – for the taste of the town.

William *The Winter's Tale* minus the first three acts?

David It's all set-up. You don't need it.

William *King Lear* with a happy ending?

David Society's advanced since Tudor times. No one wants to see an old man's misery at the closing moment of the play.

William But it *is* the closing moment of the play, it's the closing moment of every play. An old man bested, frightened, done. And curtain.

David Hey-day, you do need cheering up. How about a walk?

William What is the point of a bleeding walk without a bleeding dog? I'm tired. I'm worn out. And you seem to have forgotten that you owe me fifteen quid.

David Do I? Fifteen pounds?

William Yes.

David Alack-a-day.

William That was the price we agreed, wasn't it? For the picture of you and your Eva?

David I thought I'd paid it?

William No, you haven't paid it.

David Fifteen pounds, you say? I'm afraid I don't carry that kind of money around.

William You don't carry any kind of money around.

David There are gentlemen of the road out there! A traveller rides with caution. I shall settle at the first opportunity. Will, the price you put on 'Sigismunda' –?

William What about it?

David Bit steep, don't you think? Four hundred?

William A 'Sigismunda' went last year, to one of your connoisseurs, for exactly that sum.

David But that was a Correggio!

William It wasn't a Correggio, any fool could see it wasn't a Correggio. It was just dark, and varnished, and cracked.

Time the Destroyer had touched it. These are gullible men, they'll buy anything – as long as it's old, and foreign, and dark. My aim's to show that a British artist can produce work of the same quality as any bunch of beardy Latins. Have you heard the Society of Artists is mounting a Public Exhibition?

David Yes, I have. Highly original. Whole rooms full of pictures, for anyone to see! Why has nobody thought of that before?

William They have.

David Then why haven't we –

William They were French. They've got what they call an Academy, which says what is art, and what isn't. We won't have that bumfluff here. We are freeborn Englishmen, we can make up our own minds. The only one who subscribes to that rubbish is Reynolds, because he trained in Rome. Reynolds is intrinsically foreign. His pictures reek of garlic, and bowls of bleeding salad. Why people like him is a riddle.

David He's bought a town house near yours, am I right?

William Yeah, directly across Leicester Fields.

David What's it like?

William Big.

David They say he makes six thousand a year.

William Does he? How?

David Presumably by not sitting all day in the dark.

William Fuck off. Sir Richard Grosvenor has done me a service. He kept his money, I kept me picture. I've put 'Sigismunda' in the Public Exhibition, and stationed my man at the gallery, to listen in discreetly, and report.

I reckon that in the opinion of good honest citizens, not just some tit who owns Mayfair, my painting will be seen to be a classic exemplar of *The Analysis of Beauty*, which I'm assuming by now you have read?

David It is so brilliant, I am putting off getting to the end. I hope it will go on for ever. – Will, I'm worried about the heart in 'Sigismunda'.

William Why? It's anatomically perfect. I got it from a surgeon, who cut it from a corpse.

David But is there blood? In the picture?

William There is blood. On her fingers. There are tears. She's a person, see. She's real.

Jane enters and sees them.

Jane Oh, you have come out.

William Janey. Nice, ain't it? Sunny.

Jane Why yes.

William And that is the prettiest outfit. Doesn't she look bonny, David? Eh?

Jane (*surprised*) Oh! Thank you.

William How may I help you, princess? We are in conversation, you see.

Jane Of course. It's only that I want Samuel to drive us into town – and he's insisting on speaking to you first.

William Is he back?

Jane Yes, but I've promised Mother that we shall go shopping, so he's going to have to turn straight round, I'm afraid.

William I do need to see him. Where is he?

Jane (*calls*) Samuel! Would you come here, please?

Samuel, the coachman, enters.

William Morning, Samuel.

Samuel Good morning, sir. Oh, Mr Garrick, it's you again, good morning.

William I'm sorry you've got to go directly back to London.

Samuel It's no bother. The lad is changing the horses.

William You were at the gallery all day yesterday?

Samuel Yes. Sir, could we not speak in private?

William No, mate, we can't. Tell us what was said. Did my picture get some compliments?

Samuel Well, some of the remarks, they was favourable, and some of them, less so.

Jane Shall we just hear the nice ones?

William No, Janey, thank you. – Some was unfavourable, you say? As for instance what?

Samuel (*reads from a notebook*) 'If she ever unbends that arm, it will be two foot longer than God intended.'

William It's called foreshortening. Twat. Go on.

Samuel 'There was never a woman alive who looked like that.'

William Oh? Yes there was.

Samuel One fellow objected to the folds of her sleeves. But he was a maniac. They carted him away.

William I'll consider the sleeves. Is there more?

Samuel 'Poor Sigismunda! What a fate is thine! The helpless victim of a dauber's hand.'

William A dauber?

Samuel I think these remarks, they was not sincere, they were just made to jig up the crowd.

William By stable-boys? Apprentices?

Samuel No, by people of fashion, I am sorry to say. That last was Mr Churchill, the critic. I also saw the Duke of Nottingham, and Lady Croyde, and Mr Walpole, of Strawberry Hill.

William (*quietly*) Horace Walpole.

Jane Will –

David Horace Walpole has become influential.

William Walpoles do.

Jane Will –

William (*to David*) Do you know him?

Jane Let's not get –

David (*to William*) No. Do you?

William I knew his father. Robert. I expect young Horace had something clever to say, did he?

Jane Please –

William Hush, woman, for Christ's sake, hush!

Samuel Yes, sir. He was the centre of attention.

William gestures 'Go on'.

Well, he stands looking a long time. The room goes quiet. He puts his hand on his hip and takes two or three little steps in towards the picture, and two or three little steps out. Sort of like a peewit. Then – (*Reads from notebook.*) Sigismunda, he says, looks like 'a maudlin whore. Her fingers are bloody,' he says, 'as if she had just bought a sheep's heart in St James's market.' He finds in her 'no sober grief, no dignity of suppressed anguish, no amorous warmth turned holy by despair'.

William 'Amorous warmth'? What is he talking about?

David He is known for a charlatan.

William She's committing suicide!

David Quite.

Samuel Then he says –

Jane That's enough, thank you, Samuel. Put away your notebook. I know you are proud of it, but put it away! (*To William.*) You do not need to listen to the spite of Horace Walpole. You haven't been well. You are not strong. – Samuel, please go to the kitchen, where Cook has chicken broth. Go.

 Samuel exits. A pause.

David Hey-day, Will. We've all had bad reviews.

William You haven't. You've no idea what it's like.

David That's true. What *is* it like? Describe to me the turmoil in your breast.

William No!

Jane There's only one thing you can do. Withdraw the picture. Pop it away out of sight.

William 'Pop it away out of sight'?

David I think Jane has a point.

William I'm Serjeant-Painter to the King!

Jane And Mr Walpole is an influential critic. We do not play at hazard with our livelihood.

William But it was a personal attack. You know it and I know it. 'Sigismunda' is my greatest work!

Jane Will, it's not your greatest work. It's just not! I'm going to put Mother in the carriage.

She turns to leave.

William Put her in her casket, there's a better idea.

Jane How dare you?

William How dare I what?

Jane How dare you be so rude?

William Rude? I'm getting shat on from Strawberry Hill, and you're disappearing fucking shopping! That's what I call rude!

Jane Do not swear at me.

William All right! Off you go to the shops. Buy something nice for Mother. Some coffin-nails, perhaps? Only don't buy the short ones, she'll get out.

Jane Why are you being so childish?

William Because you're meant to be on my side!

Jane I am on your side.

William Doesn't look like it.

Jane I beg your pardon?

William Some Muse you turned out to be. I should have done another one of Trump.

Jane William, I know you miss him, but –

William Yeah, I do, he liked my work. He'd lie under the easel, wagging his tail, and never criticising nothing! Good old Trump!

Jane If you *ever* showed me the affection you showed that wretched dog! I don't know why you married me at all!

William No, it's a mystery, isn't it?

Jane Are you going to apologise for that?

William No, sorry, I ain't.

Jane Why not?

William Because I'm having a bastard day! Jane!

Jane For pity's sake, it's only a painting! (*Furiously.*) Do another one!

David bows as Jane exits.

David Go after her.

William Not likely.

David I'd go after mine.

William Yeah, but you're all codpiece, and no cod. (*Pause.*) They've turned on me, Davy. I used to be at the centre of things. Now I'm a smear in the margin. I've cocked it, good and proper.

David That is patently absurd. Consider your circumstance: a fine house in town, a fine house in the country, a good wife, albeit with a sharp tongue, and a mulberry tree in the garden. Why, Shakespeare had a mulberry tree! Shakespeare!

William Tell you what. Let's go for a walk.

David Splendid!

William We'll walk to your place at Hampton.

David I was thinking of a turn round Chiswick Park?

William No, let's walk to your place. We can stable your horse for you here.

David Will, we'll have to go all the way through Richmond and Twickenham and Bushy. Three hours at least. Must we really walk that far?

William You walked from Lichfield, didn't you? With your fat friend Johnson? Three hours is nothing to you. (*Calls.*) Bridget! (*To David.*) I'll buy you a meal in one of them inns on the river.

David Behold, I see a vision of a sirloin, very rare – garnished with horseradish, red with blood – the roast beef of old England, what?

William I'm not allowed beef no more. Bowels. Bit of bread and cheese would be nice.

David Bread and cheese it shall be! We march to Hampton! Sound trumpets, let our bloody colours wave!

He is cutting a military figure as Bridget enters.

Bridget Did you call, sir?

William Yes, Bridget.

David Aha. Fair Bridget of the West!

William Oi. Go and sort out your horse.

David I now see you as Rosalind, Bridget. If you can carry the verse.

He exits.

William I want my best coat – the brocade – and my good wig. Them shoes with the silver buckles.

Bridget Yes, sir.

William Get them laid out.

Bridget Are you off somewhere special?

William Strawberry Hill.

Bridget Oh, sir! Strawberry Hill! I hear 'tis a paradise, burnished with gold.

William Don't tell no one, all right? It's meant to be a surprise.

Bridget nods and exits.

'Burnished with gold'. Fuck my arse.

Lady Thornhill enters, in her best bonnet.

Lady Thornhill My daughter is weeping. What have you done?

William I haven't done nothing, Lady T. I don't know why she's so crabby today.

Lady Thornhill She's lonely, you clot.

William (*surprised*) Is she? (*He considers this.*) And that's my fault, I suppose?

Lady Thornhill I had a dream you went to China, and never came back. Oh it was lovely. A consoling dream, a comforter, that I shall carry at my bosom as we coach to the West End.

William To spend my money.

Lady Thornhill Your money? Bah. Jane runs the business.

William I do the paintings!

Lady Thornhill She buys the paints. She woos the clients. She balances the books. Without her you would be a nonentity. You'd be a debtor like your father, or at best engraving heraldry on cheap baronial silver. Without Jane

133

you are nothing! My daughter has given you everything, yet you can't even give her a child. What kind of husband insults his wife like that? Why, your servants you give more respect than her!

Samuel enters.

Samuel Excuse me, the carriage for My Lady is ready.

William Thanks, Samuel. You get your chicken broth?

Lady Thornhill Bah!

She exits.

Samuel Sir – if I may? – Mrs Hogarth is in some distress.

William Christ, not you as well. Take them bloody shopping!

Samuel exits. William seethes.

Bridget! Where are my clothes?

He exits.

SCENE TWO

A busy tea-shop in the West End. Jane and Lady Thornhill take tea, and cakes from a tiered stand. At an adjacent table sit Mrs Colquhoun and Mrs Ryott. They are wealthy, intellectual ladies.

Jane Will you not try your pastry, Mother?

Lady Thornhill I don't want it.

Jane It's apricock, your favourite. Or look – there's posset. You like that.

Lady Thornhill It smells of old boots. Something is wrong with me.

Jane Come now, you have enjoyed your hour at the shops. I'm sure I saw you smile at the milliner.

Lady Thornhill Nobody smiles at a milliner. I'm tired. I have a pain.

Jane Then when you've finished your tea, we shall get Samuel, and drive back to Chiswick.

Lady Thornhill (*in disgust*) Chiswick!

Jane Eat your tart.

Mrs Colquhoun leans across.

Mrs Colquhoun Excuse me – good afternoon! We have met, I feel sure. But I can't quite –

Jane Oh! – Good afternoon. Have we?

Mrs Colquhoun Have we not been introduced?

Jane Oh, I couldn't say, I –

Mrs Colquhoun Then I do beg your pardon. I am Hester Colquhoun.

Lady Thornhill (*aside to Jane*) Have we been introduced?

Mrs Colquhoun And this is Mrs Ryott.

Jane Mrs Ryott. – Where might we have we met, Mrs Colquhoun?

Mrs Colquhoun At Mrs Vesey's, I expect.

Jane I'm afraid I'm not acquainted with Mrs Vesey. – My mother, Lady Thornhill.

Mrs Colquhoun Good afternoon, My Lady.

Lady Thornhill nods curtly. Etiquette has not been observed.

Mrs Ryott Lady Thornhill. Are you well?

Lady Thornhill I fear not. All my life, I have loved a piece of cake. And now the wretched stuff betrays me.

Mrs Ryott I have yet to be betrayed by a cake.

Lady Thornhill The day will come. Your hair will moult. Your face will collapse, like butter left out in the sun. I give you six years, maybe seven.

Jane For pity's sake, Mother – (*To Mrs Ryott.*) She means nothing.

Mrs Colquhoun If not Mrs Vesey's, it must have been at another of the conversation parties.

Jane I don't think so, as I have never been to one.

Lady Thornhill Pray tell me, a conversation party, what is that?

Mrs Colquhoun It is an evening gathering, Lady Thornhill. We go to one another's houses.

Lady Thornhill Oh, you mean a card party? One has been to thousands. What do you play? Ombre? Brag?

Mrs Ryott Oh no, we do not play cards.

Lady Thornhill Then what do you do?

Mrs Ryott We talk.

Lady Thornhill Talk? All evening?

Mrs Ryott Sometimes way into the night.

Lady Thornhill But what is there to talk about, apart from what is trumps?

Jane Please excuse my mother, she is not feeling herself.

Lady Thornhill I am entirely myself, far more so than you are. (*To the ladies.*) With whom is one conversing, so deep into the night?

Mrs Colquhoun Well, My Lady, often we find ourselves in company with the great figures of the day. Last week we met Doctor Johnson, Mr Reynolds the painter, and the Provost of Eton.

Mrs Ryott And Mr Burke proposed a Philosophical Enquiry into the Sublime and the Beautiful.

Lady Thornhill Good grief.

Mrs Ryott Mr Burke knows his way around the Sublime! He and I talked for two hours.

Lady Thornhill But these are persons of substance. They have come to see your husbands, not you. I hope you gave no offence, or you will find it goes against you at home.

Mrs Ryott I did not give offence! Mr Burke was enchanted by my views. He said so, several times.

Lady Thornhill But what can you know of philosophy? You, a slip of a girl?

Mrs Colquhoun Mrs Ryott is, in fact, the author of *New Directions in Female Education*; she speaks Greek, Hebrew and Portugese; and plays the mandolin.

Mrs Ryott And my friend is justly celebrated for her translation of the Elegies of Propertius.

Mrs Colquhoun Those which are extant – he left only four volumes, as you know.

Mrs Ryott Oh yes! How I wish there were more!

Mrs Colquhoun *Cur haec in terris facies humana moratur?* ['Why does such mortal beauty exist on earth?']

> *Mrs Ryott and Mrs Colquhoun enjoy the 'joke' together. It annoys Lady Thornhill quite a bit.*

Lady Thornhill I find your lack of manners quite disturbing. First you introduce yourselves without being introduced; then you hold private intercourse in some unspeakable language. This is a tea-shop. A place for drinking tea. Not a place for vulgar self-promotion. A woman should not advertise her brain, even in the event that she discovers herself to have grown one.

Mrs Colquhoun Oh, I'm so sorry –

Lady Thornhill Good.

Mrs Colquhoun – but the one thing we will not do is ask pardon for our brilliance. What man is required to do that?

Jane Would you forgive my mother? She is from another time.

Mrs Colquhoun That is undoubtedly the case. – Still I struggle to recall where we have met?

Lady Thornhill (*aside*) Why can you not be friends with nice people, Jane?

Jane (*aside*) I think we have chanced on some of the blue-stockings that we've heard so much about. (*Aloud.*) Is it true that you gather with no ceremony, no cards, and no alcohol; that the chairs are arranged semi-circular; and anyone may stand up and speak? Is that so, Mrs Colquhoun?

Mrs Colquhoun It is. Lords and ladies mix with poets and theologians. The great with the good, the witty with the wise. The room throbs with enlightened conversation! For it is clear the world is changing.

Mrs Ryott Why don't you come?

Lady Thornhill You will do no such thing.

Jane I would like to. But I hold no great position.

Mrs Ryott We are very democratic.

Lady Thornhill groans.

Mrs Colquhoun We meet at my house in North Audley Street.

Lady Thornhill You may not attend without your husband.

Mrs Ryott Husbands aren't encouraged. They tend to inhibit the flow.

Lady Thornhill That is a disgraceful remark. Please, I have heard enough, let me drink my tea in peace. (*To Jane.*) Where is the fruit cake?

Jane I do not know.

Lady Thornhill searches through the cake-stand.

Mrs Colquhoun Lady Thornhill, with due respect to your rank, and your age, can you not see what is so deficient, so lacking in society today?

Lady Thornhill Is it fruit cake?

Mrs Colquhoun No. Where are the women, My Lady? They are quite simply absent from view. There are no female aldermen, no Justices of the Peace, no lawyers or notaries or parsons –

Lady Thornhill Parsons!

Mrs Colquhoun There are no women in any walk of public life.

Lady Thornhill Well, of course there aren't.

Mrs Colquhoun And that is why we hold our assemblies. We have no rights in law; but we do have the right to a life of the mind, and this we will uphold, as the first step to feminine liberty.

Lady Thornhill My dear, one moment, one moment please. You are clever, I see that, and nicely hung with diamonds,

but your intelligence, I cannot but notice, has outstripped
you. This preoccupation with liberty bemuses me. What
good do you think it will do? Do I not have as much liberty
now, as I could ever make use of? Why would anyone want
more? (*To Jane.*) Please, will you get me some fruit cake.
It's not as if I'm asking for the moon.

Jane rises, reluctantly going in search of cake.

Jane (*calls*) Waiter? Hallo!

Mrs Ryott suddenly gasps, looking at Jane.

Mrs Ryott Oh!

*Mrs Ryott has to suppress her giggles. She clutches
Mrs Colquhoun.*

(*Under her breath.*) It's her!

Mrs Colquhoun I beg your pardon, Katherine?

Mrs Ryott It's *her*! You know! This morning? *Her*!

*She points surreptitiously at Jane, who is attempting
to order more cake.*

Mrs Colquhoun Oh good Lord, it is.

Mrs Ryott The figure.

Mrs Colquhoun Yes!

Mrs Ryott The hair!

Both the ladies now try to stifle their laughter.

We have to escape. This minute! I cannot control myself,
Hester! Ha ha ha!

The ladies rise hastily.

Mrs Colquhoun Very nice to have met you, Lady Thornhill.
Good day. Ha ha ha!

Mrs Ryott Good day. Good day. Ha ha ha!

Jane (*looking around*) Oh! Goodbye.

Mrs Colquhoun Quick! Quick!

*Mrs Colquhoun and Mrs Ryott exit fast, unable to
contain their laughter. Jane, in some confusion,
watches them go.*
    *Lady Thornhill suddenly takes a bad turn, and
slumps in her chair. Jane doesn't notice at first.*

Jane You were so appallingly rude, I think you may have
caused those ladies to – (*A dreadful realisation.*) Or was it –?
Oh, God. God!

*Jane turns and sees her mother, who is gasping for
breath.*

Mother? What is it?

Jane hurries to her.

Mother!

Lady Thornhill (*weakly*) Did you get the cake?

Jane What's happened? Shall I fetch a doctor?

Lady Thornhill No. No doctors.

Jane (*calls*) Samuel! Samuel!

Samuel enters at a run.

Samuel Ma'am?

Jane Where's the carriage?

Samuel Round the corner. What's up?

Jane She's poorly. Can we get her in?

Samuel Yes, if you take one side, and me the other –

They help up Lady Thornhill, taking an arm each.

Jane Come along, Mother, we're going to the carriage.

Samuel That's the ticket, My Lady. Off we go.

They manage to take a very woozy Lady Thornhill to the door.

Jane Let's get you home. William will know what to do.

They exit.

SCENE THREE

A country lane near Twickenham. William – in his best clothes – and David, both somewhat the worse for wear, enter with a flagon of red port. They sing 'Heart of Oak':

William *and* **David**
    Come, cheer up, my lads, 'tis to glory we steer,
    To add something more to this wonderful year;
    To honour we call you, as freemen not slaves,
    For who are so free as the sons of the waves?

    Heart of oak are our ships,
    Jolly tars are our men,
    We always are ready –
    Steady, boys, steady –
    We'll fight and we'll conquer again and again!

They collapse, laughing.

David I declare, I have never, in the entire course of my life, consumed such a volume of red port.

William You have to have a glass of something with cheese. (*Raises the jug.*) Your good health.

David What was that last place called?

William The Perch and Pike.

David She was pretty, the girl. Oh, my.

William She was.

David And what was the one before that?

William Let me think, that was the Barley Mow.

David (*laughing*) And the one before that?

William The Ferry House at Mortlake.

David And where are we now?

William Well, that's Eel Pie Island, look. Petersham nurseries, over the river. So we must be nearly there.

David No, it's miles yet to my place.

William I am feeling a thousand times better. Bless you for dragging me out.

David My dear friend, you are cordially welcome.

William I am fortunate to have such a mate.

David And I, I too! Why do you suppose we rub along so well?

William Because we both come from nothing, and we both got on. I like that. I don't like blokes who have it gifted, served up on a platter. I can't sit at table with them. Nor do I know how you can.

David So I sup with lords and ladies? Well, how came I to their banquets? Was it not entirely by my sweat, perseverance, raw talent, and rugged good looks? I don't feel I've anything to be embarrassed about.

William I don't get embarrassed. I just want to hit someone. You ever run across Josh Reynolds, whilst you're stuffing your face?

David He is to be found in all the best houses.

William You talk to him?

David Certainly not. Something of a social climber, Reynolds.

William (*agreeing*) They're queuing up to overpay him for a portrait. He's nicked all the decent commissions.

David I thought you'd abandoned portraits? To concentrate on the Sublime?

William I am out of sorts with the Sublime.

David I blame you not a jot. Sublimity is all very well, if you like that kind of thing. But it's not what we are after in the theatre.

William What are you after in the theatre?

David The verity of life. The deeper truth. And forty per cent of the house.

William That's a bit cynical. My friend Fielding thought you could use the playhouse to bring down governments.

David Henry Fielding's dead. And who today remembers a single one of his plays? For all their fury, all their barbs, they made no difference whatsoever. The theatre is for entertainment; it has no political function.

William You reckon?

David People's lives are hard. Why deny them an hour or two of the pleasure of looking at me? I have a new idea for Drury Lane. I am going to hide the lights.

William Eh?

David I am going to place the stage lights out of sight.

William Think anybody will come, if there ain't no lights?

David Oh, my, yes, there will be lights! But you won't see the source of them. The scene on stage will look very much more real.

William How are you going to do that?

David I aspire to naturalness in acting, I do not aspire to excellence in physics. We have fellows in jerkins for that kind of thing. In other words, I've no idea. But a player need no longer stand rooted and declaim, like that great tree over there. He may simply *be*!

William That's fucking brilliant, mate.

David Thanks.

They are sitting on the ground and sharing the port.

William What *is* that great tree over there?

David That is an elm.

William He is a fine old elm.

David He is. Cheers!

William Cheers! To the elm!

They toast the elm.

Often wish I'd had children.

David Do you? I don't.

William Why not?

David No time.

William I could've brought them along to see this. The water meadows, Father Thames, the church spire in the distance. The moorhens and the reedbeds and the massive fucking elms. This is what I call Sublime.

David Perhaps you should paint nature?

William Fuck off, who wants to paint nature? Where's the fun in that?

David There is no comic value in a tree?

William Not much. A bush perhaps?

David (*laughs*) How about a haystack?

William Always got a milkmaid in a haystack. You basically can't go wrong. Shall we have a little rest?

David I think I could essay a little rest.

William I never used to need one. Not before.

David You have worked hard, Will. Surely you may take your ease, on a warm afternoon by the river?

They lie down.

William Fucking Titian never took a little rest.

David I know, but look what happened to him.

William Total failure.

David Laughing stock.

They giggle softly, and drift off to sleep.
Zachariah Blunt enters. He is an ex-soldier fallen on hard times. He wears the tattered remains of his uniform. One leg is withered, and he hobbles on a makeshift crutch. He surveys the sleeping men, then limps towards them cautiously. He bends over David, and puts his hand in his coat pocket. But William has woken and seen him.

William If you're looking for his purse, you're going to be disappointed.

Zachariah jumps up as best he can. David wakes.

David What ho? Stand to!

William kicks Zachariah's crutch from under him. Zachariah goes down. William grabs the crutch, and raises it high, with the intention of bringing it down on Zachariah's head.

Zachariah Sir! Don't!

David Don't hit him, Will!

Zachariah That's it, don't hit him, Will!

William lowers the crutch, but keeps it at the ready.

William What are you up to?

Zachariah I'm hungry, your honour, that's all!

David And you would steal my money, would you?

Zachariah Just tuppence for a loaf!

William He ain't got tuppence.

Zachariah I didn't mean no harm, sirs!

William You was robbing us!

Zachariah I haven't eaten.

William Oh, haven't you? We have. We had sharp cheese, with onions. And a pickled egg.

David Hogy, the man is a wreck. Show pity.

Zachariah I don't want your pity. See this uniform? I'm a Fusilier, thank you very much!

William Well, I'm a Serjeant, so you're outranked.

Zachariah A Sergeant? No you're never.

William I am Serjeant-Painter to the King. I have his commission. And two hundred pound a year for the privilege.

Zachariah King George the Third?

William King George the Third.

Zachariah God save His Majesty! They say he can speak English. Which is uncommon, don't you think? Why, you have to go back to Queen Anne for –

William Look, nobody asked for a history lesson, knob-head.

David Will, Will. Shall we spoil a convivial outing with tumults and alarums? – What is your name, Fusilier?

Zachariah My name is Zachariah Blunt, sir.

David And where have you fought?

Zachariah In India. Down the Coromandel Coast.

David With Colonel Clive?

Zachariah That's it, Hundred-and-Second Regiment of Foot, British East India Company.

David Then I salute you, Mr Blunt. Will, we have in our midst a hero of Plassey and Chandernagar! (*To Zachariah.*) Your victories are trumpeted from the rooftops, lauded to the skies! You have driven the French out of India, and opened the door to trade!

Zachariah I didn't do it on me own.

David You played your part! Who can do more? We offer our gratitude. This is Mr Hogarth, and I am David Garrick.

Zachariah Come off it. You're not David Garrick. I've seen David Garrick on the stage.

William Was he any good?

Zachariah He was magnificent, and that's no lie!

David I am he.

Zachariah No you're not.

David Forsooth, I am he.

Zachariah If you're David Garrick, you're going to have to prove it.

David I don't think I have to prove that I am myself.

William Seems a reasonable request.

Zachariah You look not a bit like Garrick. He is a colossus of a man. I saw him give his Macbeth.

David I'd rather you didn't say that.

William It's all right, we ain't in a theatre.

David It is true that I have played the tragic Scot.

Zachariah Fearsome, it was! I barely slept a wink that night! I will never forget the agony of his dying, as I witnessed it at Drury Lane. If you're David Garrick, as you claim to be, give us the final moments of Macbeth.

David Sir, were we in a theatre, I should require you to leave the building, spit, curse, spin around three times, and beg to be allowed back in.

Zachariah Do what?

David Never mention that word again.

Zachariah What, Macb—

David Silence!

He prepares to 'enter' as Macbeth.

Now, the King is mortally wounded, his broadsword broke in two.

William (*groans*) Oh, you're not going to –

David This is a man disabled in the service of his country! Does he not deserve, perhaps more than most, the consolations of dramatic art? – Did you take shot in your leg?

Zachariah No, your honour. I was stood upon by an armoured elephant. They can get skittish in a battle.

David Thus we treat our fighting men, in this unfeeling age. We send them off to foreign wars, there to be butchered and maimed, mangled, bloodied, and destroyed, until homewards they plod, or limp, or crawl, sufferers of mental torment, dry husks of warriors, cast out, abandoned, and forlorn.

Zachariah It's just me leg.

David Well, soldier, I give you the climax of the Scottish play, in honour of your wounds. You were high in the gallery, at the Lane, I expect?

Zachariah I was, way up in the gods.

David Today, Mr Blunt, you are seated in a box upon the stage. If you please.

He invites Zachariah to sit.

William I can't believe I'm seeing this.

David The King enters, alone.

William Where's the other fellow – Macduff?

David The King enters, alone.
''Tis done! The scene of life will quickly close.
Ambition's vain, delusive dreams are fled,

And now I wake to darkness, guilt and horror
I cannot bear it! Let me shake it off.
'Twa not be; my soul is clogged with blood.
I cannot rise! I dare not ask for mercy.
It is too late, hell drags me down. I sink,
I sink – Oh! – My soul is lost forever! Oh!'

*And here's a contemporary account of how Garrick
played this scene:*

'*His eyes became dim, his voice could not support the
efforts he made to speak his thoughts. His gestures
revealed the approach of the last moment; his legs gave
way under him, his face lengthened, his pale and livid
features bore the signs of suffering and repentance. At
last, he fell; his crimes peopled his thoughts with the
most horrible forms; terrified at the hideous picture
which his past acts revealed to him, he struggled against
death. He clawed the ground and seemed to be digging
his own grave.*'

*And thus, he 'dies'. A long silence. Zachariah is awed.
David dusts himself down.*

William Who actually wrote that?

David I did.

William It didn't *sound* like Shakespeare.

Zachariah Mr Garrick, I owe you an apology!

David Shakespeare isn't flawless, as I've told you many
times.

Zachariah That was better than Shakespeare.

David (*to Zachariah*) Oh, better? (*To William.*) Better,
quoth he! (*To Zachariah.*) Could you enlarge upon that
thought?

Zachariah Why, that was as real as real could be! I have seen men die in the field. I have seen them claw the earth as they expired – and Bengal earth, at that. I have seen the horror on their faces, like what I seen on yours, as they bled out, scratching at the dirt. You catch the moment perfect – fighting men on their way to hell. You are a genius, sir, and I am in your debt. But who this geezer is I'm none the wiser.

David This is William Hogarth, Mr Blunt. A most important artist. Surely you have heard of him?

Zachariah (*thinks*) I've heard of Joshua Reynolds.

William still has Zachariah's crutch. He readies it.

William Are you on the parish?

Zachariah No. The parish give me me marching orders. The words 'apple' and 'bad' was deployed in the very same sentence.

William Then how do you live?

Zachariah I knock at back doors, get scrapings and leavings, sometimes I tickle a trout.

William A poacher?

Zachariah I might have been, till some bloody elephant sat on me knee. No, I just beg, mate. I beg.

William Ever begged at the kitchen of Strawberry Hill?

Zachariah That weird place? What we call The Castle?

William It's not far from here, is it?

Zachariah Half-mile or so.

David Will, we are not going to Strawberry Hill.

William I thought we'd drop in, since we're close?

David What demented fancy grips your brain? We are not intruding on the peace of Horace Walpole!

William That is frankly unsociable, David. Are you telling me we have walked all this way for nothing?

David I thought you wanted to talk to me!

William I have talked to you. Now I want to talk to Mr Walpole.

David Then I regret, I may accompany you no further.

William Busy, are we?

David Eva awaits me at the villa.

William I thought she was in town?

David She left town. She's at the villa.

William With her spaniel snuffling in her lap? I'd keep an eye on the little fucker, if I were you.

David I will not discompose Mr Walpole! He is a Member of Parliament!

William This morning you called him a charlatan!

David The man's entitled to privacy, charlatan or no! And do not talk like that about my wife! (*To Zachariah.*) I thank you for your measured and insightful criticism, Mr Blunt. Ask for me at the playhouse. We'll give you a backstage tour.

Zachariah You're not leaving me with *him*?

David I fear I am the victim of some subterfuge, alas. Sirs.

He bows and exits fast.

William David! I thought we were friends? Where are you going? Oi, Dave! (*Calls after him.*) Hearts of oak!

Remember? You should do, you wrote the bloody song!
Hearts of oak! Jolly tars! – Jesus Christ.

Zachariah is trying to shuffle away, without his
crutch. Will notices.

Where the fuck are you going, hoppy?

Zachariah My wife also awaits for me at the villa, as it
goes.

William No she doesn't. (*Laughs.*) Relax, mate. I'm not
going to hurt you. Do you know a way in to Strawberry
Hill?

Zachariah Might do.

William Could be a consideration, if you did.

Zachariah Go past the cloister. There's a little window, left
of the scullery door. The catch is bust.

William Thanks.

He takes out his purse and gives a small coin to
Zachariah, who isn't impressed.

Zachariah What's this?

William A tanner.

Zachariah A tanner?

William What did you expect?

Zachariah You said a reward!

William A consideration, I said. Sixpence is enough. You're
lucky I ain't called the Constable, you thieving little turd.

He starts to leave, with the crutch.

(*To Zachariah.*) I'll leave this at the next stile I come to.

Zachariah You can't do that.

William This way, is it? Strawberry Hill?

He exits.

Zachariah Don't leave me here! I'm disabled! From marauding down the Coromandel Coast!

Nothing. Zachariah puts his fingers to his mouth and blows a piercing whistle. A moment later Nancy comes cautiously towards him – a young woman wrapped in a cloak. She has the cowl up over her head; we don't see her face.

Help us up, for fuck's sake.

Nancy helps Zachariah to his feet.

Nancy You all right?

Zachariah No, I'm not. I have had my dignity besmirched. As also the honour of the Regiment. You do not do that to the Hundred-and-Second. We cut off your fucking ears. (*Roars.*) You hear me? You do not that to Zachariah Blunt!

They start to follow William, Zachariah leaning on Nancy.

After him. Strawberry Hill!

They exit.

End of Act One.

Act Two

The Long Gallery at Strawberry Hill House. Paintings line the walls. We hear a distant crash and a tinkle of glass; then William enters, triumphant, but not very steady on his feet.

William I think I've got my second wind. That is the beauty of alcohol. Just as you're about to do something very stupid, you have a little pause, and you have a little drink, and then you think fuck it, and do it.

He looks around.

It is ages since I acted like a tit. I feel like a soul resurrected. (*Yells.*) Walpole! Where are you? Oi, Horace!

His eye is caught by a painting.

Here, is that a Rembrandt?

He examines the painting. Mrs Bascombe, the housekeeper, enters and watches him from a distance.

The bastard's got a Rembrandt. A Giorgione. And if I'm not mistaken, a Watteau. And who's this?

Mrs Bascombe It is Annibale Carracci, the master of Bologna.

William Oh, Carracci, is it?

Mrs Bascombe A good example of early mannerism. Have you lost the tour?

William Pardon?

Mrs Bascombe The guided tour is in the Holbein Chamber.

William I'm not with the tour.

Mrs Bascombe Have you a ticket? Mr Walpole issues tickets, for curious persons.

William No, I think it must be in my other coat.

Mrs Bascombe My instructions say: 'No ticket will serve but on the day for which it is given. If more than four persons come with a ticket, the housekeeper' – which that is me – 'has orders to admit none of them.' Think, then, sir, what my orders might be, for a person in Strawberry Hill *without no ticket*!

William If you wouldn't mind, Mrs, I'm working.

Mrs Bascombe exits with a huff. William views another picture.

That's a Poussin. Now that is impressive.

William considers the painting closely. Mrs Bascombe comes back with Horace Walpole – forties, effete, beautifully dressed, but limping. Mrs Bascombe points out William.

Look at the flesh tones! The brushwork on the goats!

Horace (*approaching*) Yes, he can do goats, can't he? How are you with goats?

William Dismal, mate. Awful.

Horace May I ask what brings you to my little Gothick castle?

William I just wanted a look at your Poussin.

Horace You are not the first. It is called 'The Nurture of Jupiter'. It cost a hundred and fourteen pounds.

William Fucking worth it, Christ. What a collection!

Horace Mr Hogarth, we are honoured by your visit.

William I come in through a window. Round the back.

Horace The door is open, dear friend. My companions at the club must petition for a ticket, or force their way in if they will; but the Royal Serjeant-Painter may have ingress as he pleases.

William I broke into your home. Aren't you cross?

Horace No.

William Why not?

Horace My greatest ambition is never to grow cross. You will take some refreshment, I hope?

William The thing is, Mr Walpole, I harbour a complaint!

Horace I'm most grateful. The afternoon was passing very slow.

William You what?

Horace My dear, belligerent fellow, do sit down. Some tea? Or something stronger? – Bring, I think, the grappa, Mrs Bascombe.

Mrs Bascombe Which that is locked in the library?

Horace Yes.

Mrs Bascombe exits.

Will you sit? I must.

William Why?

Horace I am riven with the gout, sir, in the linkage of my knee.

William Yeah? My guts are like Dante's Inferno.

Horace Then God preserve the pair of us. Sit down, I beg you, that I may, too.

They sit.

We are neighbours, are we not?

William I have a place at Chiswick.

Horace Ah, Chiswick.

William It ain't a bit like this.

Horace Strawberry Hill is unique. I adore the Middle Ages, and the Dark Ages, oh and the lovely Renaissance, in fact every century up to the one before last, and I've brought them all together under one great pinnacled roof. Do look. Overhead you see a fan-vaulted ceiling, modelled on Henry the Seventh's chapel at Westminster. Richer than the roof of paradise! The fireplaces are in the medieval manner, likewise the quatrefoil windows, and the ogees over the doors. It is a style I call gloomth.

William Eh?

Horace A mixture of gloom and warmth. Gloomth! Exquisite, don't you agree? I begin to be ashamed of my magnificence.

William Yeah, I would be.

Horace Strawberry is the creation of myself and my most intimate friends – the Committee of Taste. Who did yours?

William looks blank.

Your house, who designed it?

William Oh, my wife, she does the decorating.

Horace How charming that must be – a wife, a little wife. A helpmeet. A spouse. I've only Mrs Bascombe for company.

Horace smiles at Mrs Bascombe as she enters with drinks on a tray.

Mrs Bascombe You have all them parties.

Horace We do have parties, yes we do! Our little masquerades!

He claps his hands happily. Mrs Bascombe offers William a drink. He sniffs it suspiciously.

William What's this?

Horace I import it from Friuli.

Mrs Bascombe It's strong. Be warned.

William We have strong drink in Middlesex, you know.

He drains it in one. He gasps for breath.

Christ, that is definitely foreign.

Horace You won't take another one, surely?

William You suggesting I can't hold it? Same again.

He offers his glass. Mrs Bascombe exits with it.

Horace Have you ever been to Italy?

William No. I went to Calais once, it was a nightmare, I come directly back.

Horace I adore France. And Florence, and Rome. But Twickenham is my fastness, the Thames my tranquil vale. What is it you wish to discuss?

William 'Sigismunda'.

Horace First let me show you some curiosities. I have several excellent relics. The hair of Mary Tudor in a locket. The solid gold armour of Francis the First, and the shaffron for his horse. But I was outbid for Oliver Cromwell's nightcap, damn my luck.

William You said 'Sigismunda' was –

Horace Or would you like to see the garden? The river winds most intelligently through those willows.

William Look, I'm trying to start an argument –

Horace Yes, I'm looking forward to it –

William – and you keep butting in!

Horace I'm surprised you've the time to go quarrelling, with a brand new King on the throne. The Serjeant-Painter's duties must be onerous. New coats-of-arms on all the barges, chariots, tents, pavilions, trumpet-banners –

William I don't do that myself! I have blokes.

Horace Oh, it's a sinecure? I didn't know. I thought you suffered days and days of unicorns and *fleurs-de-lys* and – (*Pause.*) I also have one or two sinecures. On graduating from Cambridge I became Usher of the Exchequer, three thousand nine hundred per annum, then Clerk of the Escheats, and Comptroller of the Pipe. From my father I got the Collectorship of the Customs, oh, and Member of Parliament for Callington, which I believe is in Cornwall, though I've never set foot in the place. How much do you make as Serjeant-Painter?

William I don't do it for the money.

Horace Quite. Who does? Have you met the King?

William No, I haven't met the King! Have you?

Horace I saw him last week in the levee-room, squawking something that passes for English. He will invigorate the nation, if he ain't led astray by Mr Pitt. We have seen too much war, don't you agree? But we keep winning battles. Our bells are worn threadbare with the ringing of victories. But the lives! The lives it will cost! This drive to enslave the world! I despise it – and the merchants who clamour for it, too. Say what you will about my father, he kept us at peace, and we prospered.

William Well, *he* prospered.

Horace He died, in fact, in a blizzard of debt. All of his pictures will have to be sold. The Empress of Russia is keen. But of course, I remember, you worked for my father, did you not?

William I never worked for Robert Walpole.

Horace He said you did. Some silverware?

William I don't know what you're talking about.

Horace No matter: he's in his mausoleum now, in Norfolk. He lies with my mother, and his mistress, too – a sweet little *ménage* in heaven. Are your parents still – ?

William No, they're gone.

Horace Do you miss them?

William I've never stopped to think. One day they was there, the next they was gone.

Horace And where are they entombed?

William Entombed? My old chap died a pauper. He's in a common grave in Smithfield, by St Bart's. My mother got a decent send-off, though.

> *Mrs Bascombe returns with another grappa for William.*

Horace My mother was an angel.

William Yeah, mine too. Somewhat liberal with a left hook, but angelic, nonetheless.

Horace Let us drink to them: our dear, departed parents.

William All right. If you will.

Horace Mater and Pater.

William Mum and Dad.

Horace *Salut.*

William Cheerio.

William drains his glass. Horace sips his.

You could get a taste for this, once you overcome the sense of being poisoned.

Horace Please fetch the bottle, Mrs B.

Mrs Bascombe Which that has cost seven guineas?

Horace This afternoon we sacrifice to Bacchus.

Mrs Bascombe huffs and leaves.

Now, you mention your attempt at 'Sigismunda' –

William You were downright rude about it, mate. I don't know what it is you hold against me.

Horace I hold nothing whatever against you. You are one of my favourite artists.

William Am I?

Horace Sir, you are a great and original genius. Why else would I collect you?

William You collect me?

Horace Yes, I have some etchings, oh, and I have the picture of that murderess, that you did in Newgate Gaol – the day before she hanged.

William How did you get that?

Horace Came up at auction. Not awfully dear.

William It bloody well should be, it cost me some grief! I had to paint it in secret and –

Horace Did you? Why so?

William Well, my wife was on the warpath, and –

Horace Oh, do tell! I love to know the provenance of everything I own.

William Now look here, Mr Walpole. You called 'Sigismunda' a tart. That's personal, that's a personal affront.

Horace I fail to see why.

William You know exactly why.

Horace If I have offended, I do apologise. I was in the dullest of humours, for my darling Rosette had just died.

William Rosette? Who's Rosette?

Horace My little dog.

William You lost your dog?

Horace Yes.

William Oh. That's bad luck.

Horace Yes.

William Fond of her, was you?

Horace Devoted.

William Well, I'm sorry to hear it.

Horace I shall never love anyone again.

William No, I know what you mean.

Horace Have you also –?

William Yeah. My Trump. He was a character.

Horace Was he a good dog? Was he?

William He was a blinder. Never lost a scrap. As they say, the more I see of people, the more I like my dog.

Horace Quite! Quite! My heart is worn out with the baseness and treachery I have met with all my life. It is suspicious, and doubtful, and cooled. All it had for comfort was Rosette.

William Do you think you'll get another?

Horace (*bursts into tears*) Oh, don't be silly!

Mrs Bascombe enters with the grappa. She gives William a withering look as she pours his drink. Horace snuffles.

William Look, I didn't know about Rosette. I'm sorry for barging in like I done.

Horace I'm glad of the company. Let us drink Italian spirits, and be merry!

Horace holds out his glass, and Mrs Bascombe refills it. William is now a bit teary, too.

William How can we be merry? We've got two dead dogs.

Horace My darling Rosette.

William Good old Trump. Never lost a fight.

They both weep.

Horace But we must be cheerful, my friend! We must! We have to consider everything as a source of amusement, for if we looked at it seriously, we should pretty soon detest the world.

William You're right. Can't have grown men going around crying, can you?

Horace No, you can't.

William Bloody dogs.

They pull themselves together, blowing their noses.

Horace Thankfully one will always find something to laugh at. Mrs Bascombe, for instance, who's convinced that she understands painting.

Mrs Bascombe I understand as much as he does. (*Meaning William.*)

Horace D'you see? Being daily exposed to great art, she thinks she grasps its deepest secrets. Without any schooling at all! Hilarious!

Mrs Bascombe Oh, I'm satirical now, am I?

Horace Yes, dear, you are! – There's a subject for you, Hogarth: 'Mrs Bascombe's Guide to the Late Renaissance'. What do you say?

Mrs Bascombe slams the bottle down between them, and turns away, in a strop. Horace is laughing.

William I've given up the comical stuff.

Horace Oh, but why? I do so love your work.

William Then why do you abuse it?

Horace Well, I cannot be seen to show bias, for the town hangs on my judgement. They call me the Prime Minister of Taste. I can hardly stand dumb in the face of incompetence, can I?

William What do you mean, incompetence?

Horace You cannot be unaware of the technical faults of 'Sigismunda'?

Apparently William is.

The poor woman swivels at an impossible angle. Has she some pelvic deformity? The right arm is too long. The fingers are too long. The hand does not touch the head it is meant to be supporting. The goblet containing the repulsive heart might be leant upon her bosom, or it might be half a yard distant, who knows? And the face! Your model's face is not a classical face. It is ugly.

William What?

Horace Dear friend, retrocede from history and myth. Embrace your caricaturas.

William Did you say ugly?

Horace Dear Hogarth, I rather think of you as a writer of comedy with a pencil, than as a painter.

William But I am a painter!

Horace You will never be a great one. Your colouring is infirm. Your grasp of depth is minimal, your composition uncontrolled. Forgive me, I bear no malice. But the genius that enters so feelingly into your calamities of everyday life deserts you in a walk that calls for dignity and grandeur.

William The Sublime.

Horace Exactly so.

William A fucking stupid idea in the first place.

Horace Allow me the honour of buying your painting.

William What?

Horace Sell 'Sigismunda' to me. I understand Dick Grosvenor has refused it?

William The price is four hundred.

Horace Pounds or guineas?

William Guineas. That was what was paid for that Correggio last year.

Horace It wasn't a Correggio, though, was it, Mrs B?

Mrs Bascombe No. We have a Magdalene of Correggio. It was nothing like. I believe it to have been a Furini.

William It still sold for four hundred quid!

Horace But you are not a Correggio, nor even a Furini. You are Hogarth, of Smithfield Market, the odour of livestock still fresh on your clothes. I will pay your price for this poor effort, since it will be worth much more in years to come – unlike my gingerbread castle, which will soon blow away in the wind. Oh, it looks like stone, but it's actually rough-cast plaster on a timber frame, done by some strapping lads from Teddington. Strawberry cannot last. Nothing will last. Perhaps if I had children? But I have none. Nor you, I understand. So all we leave behind us is our art, our hesitant, fretful, fragile works of art. Wait here whilst I write out my cheque.

> *Horace exits. William takes another look at the paintings.*

William Who's your favourite, then, Mrs Bascombe?

Mrs Bascombe Living or dead?

William Let's say living.

Mrs Bascombe Joshua Reynolds, of course.

William Well, I walked into that. It is me who is Serjeant-Painter to His Majesty, you know.

Mrs Bascombe But it is Mr Reynolds who's revitalised English painting, and made portraiture high art. Did you know he is an enthusiast for chemistry?

William Is he really.

Mrs Bascombe Yes, he's trying to find the chromatic palette of Veronese, Tintoretto. He experiments with pigments. He even makes his own glazes!

William Which crack, about five minutes later.

Mrs Bascombe He paints in the Grand Manner. He has action, movement, scale. And he flatters his audience. His patrons look up at the pictures they've bought, and what do they see? Themselves! As gods and goddesses! Conquerors of the world! No one wants gin and starvation, poxy fat whores. The new thing is to delve inside the brain, and find out who we are.

William But I know who I am!

Mrs Bascombe Do you?

William Look. My art's not some doorway to the soul, some kind of beautifying mirror.

Mrs Bascombe Perhaps it ought to be, which then you might be as popular as Mr Reynolds. David Garrick was describing his latest, when he was here last Sunday. It has a scheme of brilliance, he says.

William What do you mean, when he was here last Sunday?

Mrs Bascombe Oh, excuse me, I understood Mr Garrick to be a friend of yours.

William Yes, he is, but –

Mrs Bascombe Yes, he often talks of you. (*Smiles to herself.*) Anyhow, on this occasion he was telling us of the wonderful portrait that Mr Reynolds has embarked on.

William What – wait a minute – David Garrick was *here*?

Mrs Bascombe His villa is just yonder, sir, at Hampton.

William Does he come often?

Mrs Bascombe Not often, no. Just for lunch on Sundays.

William I feel a bit sick.

Mrs Bascombe No one is sick in Strawberry Hill, sir. Please.

William What's this picture? Tell me.

Mrs Bascombe Which that is called 'Garrick between Comedy and Tragedy'. Mr Reynolds has referenced the 'Judgement of Hercules' of not one, but two Old Masters. From Guido Reni he takes his Tragedy; from Correggio, his Comedy. A man between two ladies. Which to choose? Virtue or vice? High art or low? In one fell swoop he has caught David Garrick's complexity. It's ingenious. Just two more sittings, Garrick says.

William Two more sittings? To Joshua Reynolds?

Mrs Bascombe Yes, at his house in town, which is, apparently –

William – fucking enormous, yes, I know.

Horace returns, drying the ink on a piece of paper, which he then hands to William.

Horace My promissory note. Four hundred guineas. Mrs Bascombe will arrange transportation.

William You don't have a Reynolds here, do you?

Horace Certainly not. Terrible show-off.

William Well, if 'Sigismunda' hangs with this lot, she will be in good company, I reckon.

Horace Yes, she would, indeed she would. But in fact I may display her in a shop in Piccadilly.

William A shop? In Piccadilly?

Horace In the window, as a lesson to the overweening artist. Stray not from your true path.

William But – you can't put it up in public, so they can point and stare and – You can't!

Horace I now own the picture. It is mine. I believe I may do as I like.

William But I will be a laughing stock!

Horace How you must weary of it.

William What?

Horace Take my advice: go back to caricaturas. You have failed at everything else.

William What?

Horace For the love of God, man, make us laugh!

William Now, you can just – you condescending – you can just – you insult me, sir!

Horace You have in your hand a cheque for four hundred guineas. If that's an insult, it's an awful expensive one.

William, outmanoeuvred, can't think of a response. He tears up the promissory note, in a fury.

William Right! Right! Fuck the fucking lot of you! My picture ain't for sale! Goodbye!

William exits. They wait to see if he's coming back. But no. Horace breathes a sigh of relief.

Horace He's gone!

Mrs Bascombe You have done that most delicate, sir.

Horace Oh, thank you. I thought he might bite me, when he arrived.

Mrs Bascombe He's as drunk as a lord. I wouldn't like to be him when he gets home.

Horace Ooh, no. The wife is a shrew, by all accounts.

Mrs Bascombe Would you really have paid four hundred?

Horace For her? No.

They exit.

SCENE FIVE

A jetty on the River Thames at Twickenham. William enters.

William (*to himself*) He made me drink a toast to Robert Walpole. Clever bastard. How did he do that?

He sees a boat. He waves.

Hey! Boatman! You for hire?

Boatman (*off*) Where are you headed, guv'nor?

William Mortlake!

Boatman (*off*) Sorry, we're going upriver!

William Right. I'll wait then.

William sits disconsolately. We become aware of Nancy, loitering nearby. She wears a low-cut bodice and has an earthenware bottle of gin. William doesn't see her.

David, David, what have you done? First you fawn on Horace Walpole behind my back. Then this gross pernicious treason with the fucking arsehole Reynolds. And I thought we were mates! This is what you learn as you get older: don't trust no one. No one! On your way up, you blaze like a comet, they adore you. But wait till your fiery tail's gone cold, wait till you're dropping like spent ordnance, down through an empty sky – look around, mate, see who's left.

Nancy approaches him.

Nancy Waiting for a boat?

William No, I'm waiting for the second coming, what does it look like?

Nancy I don't mind a second coming, now and then.

William (*laughs*) What you got in the bottle?

Nancy offers it. William drinks.

Tastes like the stuff I wash me brushes with.

Nancy It's gin.

William Yeah, I've heard of it. Thanks.

He hands it back.

Nancy What's your name, then?

William William. Yours?

Nancy Nancy. That's a nice coat you've got on. Are you out for a treat? I could give you a treat.

William You're a girl of the game, Nance, are you?

Nancy Something wrong with that?

William No. Just don't expect to find you lot round here. Seven Dials, Vauxhall, Kingston town on a Saturday night, pissing in the gutter with a pork chop in your hand, that's your territory. But out in the sticks? The pastoral idyll? No.

Nancy Had a bad day, have you, love?

William Why do you say that?

Nancy You sound upset.

William Ah, well, you know. The slings and arrows, or some bollocks. (*Pause.*) Look, what I do is, I show the world to itself, in all its foul complexions. The Dutch do it, no one complains – a bit of wassailing and whatnot, we think it's picturesque. I do it, I'm an ape with a pencil, a freak in a booth at Bartholomew fair, with a sign: 'The English Painter'. They don't like it, Nance. They don't like me. They think I'm a Low Comedian. A Smithfield boy in a velvet coat, who has not learnt his station.

Nancy squeezes up close to him.

Nancy Sounds awful. – I can make you feel better.

William Sorry, I've got to get home.

Nancy There isn't a boat.

William I'm married. I've been true to my wife for years and years.

Nancy In which case you'll be ready for a little go with Nancy, won't you, duck? Be like a magazine of powder, ready to explode. What do you say?

William I'd rather have a lie down, to be honest. My head's throbbing.

Nancy Lie down with me, I'll make something throb. I'll make you harder than the Devil's own dick.

William (*laughs*) I don't think there's much chance of that. Time the Destroyer has touched it. It ain't the great engine of formerly.

Nancy Put it about, did you, Will?

William I believe I did, my darling. Up and down the colonnades of Covent Garden late at night. In and out the *bagnios*. Blimey.

The memory brings a smile to his face.

This is when I was young.

Nancy But now you're married. And Mrs Will won't take it in the mouth.

William She won't take it anywhere.

Nancy I'll take it anywhere. Firm as an apple, look. Tight as a vice.

William How much?

Nancy Ten bob.

William That's a lot.

Nancy You can afford it.

She fingers his splendid coat.

Come down the riverbank. I know a spot.

William There's people around.

Nancy No there ain't. Just swans. Come with Nancy.

She takes his hand and leads him down to the foreshore. He looks around, and follows.

William Can I touch?

Nancy Where's your money?

William jangles his purse, then puts it back in his pocket. Nancy allows him to touch her body.

William I haven't felt one of these for years. Little nipples sticking up.

Nancy What else is sticking up, I wonder?

Nancy puts her hand inside William's breeches.

William Oh, God.

William slips his coat off, and drops it on the ground.

That's it. Go on.

Nancy works hard with her hand, but to no avail.

Nancy Nothing's happening, duck.

William Keep trying. It needs some encouragement, that's all.

Nancy Needs a fucking miracle, I reckon. (*She gives up.*) Nah. Waste of time.

William No, it ain't – come on –

Nancy Nah, it is. You couldn't shag a suet pudding with that.

William Oh, thanks, you've made my day.

Nancy Had too much drink, haven't you? You shouldn't at your age. Just give me the money and we'll leave it.

William Give you the money? For what?

Nancy You had a good feel.

William I want more than a feel for ten bob.

Nancy You're past it, duck. You're decrepit.

William Oi, that's enough. Behave.

William picks up his coat. Zachariah Blunt enters behind him.

Nancy Why? You dirty old git. You filthy old fucker.

William Don't speak to me like that! I'm important!

Nancy Oh, you are, are you?

William I'll have you know I'm William Hogarth, Serjeant-Painter to the King!

Zachariah inches towards William on his crutch.

Nancy Oh yeah? I had a bloke an hour ago, he said he was David Garrick! Pay me my ten shillings!

William If you think you're getting half a quid for a –

Zachariah lifts his crutch and smashes it down on William's head. William buckles. Zachariah hits him again. William lies still.

Zachariah (*to William*) I told you. You do not take liberties with Zachariah Blunt. Get his shoes, Nance.

Nancy What took you so long?

Zachariah laughs unpleasantly. Nancy pulls off William's shoes. Zachariah takes his coat.

Zachariah Run for it! Quick!

They exit.
    William is left bloodied in the mud in his shirt and stockings. His wig has fallen off. He groans. Then he loses consciousness.
    Lady Thornhill enters, above. She has her parasol, as if taking her afternoon constitutional.

Lady Thornhill La, there he is. – I thought I'd find you here.

William stirs. He sees her.

William Lady Thornhill –?

Lady Thornhill Why are you lying in the mud?

William I've been cudgelled, Lady T!

Lady Thornhill Bah. Where is your dignity? Up, oaf! Stand!

William I can't. I'm bleeding. My head –

Lady Thornhill Then crawl.

William crawls towards her.

Come along! One does not have all day.

With difficulty, William crawls to her feet. She spits on him.

William Oi! What was that for?

Lady Thornhill I hear you enjoy humiliation.

William Who told you that?

Lady Thornhill I hope it's true, as we are only just beginning.

William Why, what have I done?

Lady Thornhill You have failed the great test of life. You cannot give your woman a child. You are a capon, a gelding, a sapless, blighted tree.

William Loads of people can't have children!

Lady Thornhill What people? No one I know!

William Look, I tried!

Lady Thornhill Oh, you tried? What happened? Was there only pox inside your withered, shrunken balls?

William That's a bit personal, isn't it?

Lady Thornhill My line ends here. I shall have no posterity, and you, Master Hogarth, are the cause. Hide your face. Put it in the slime of the Thames. You disgust me.

William I know, but do I really have to –

Lady Thornhill Hide from my wrath, boy! Hide!

William does as he's told, and lies prostrate.

But vengeance is mine, saith the Lord. For I have found the rat-bait in the cellar. I have found the dog bowl full of meat.

William What?

Lady Thornhill He always was a greedy devil, Trump.

William No! Not Trump!

Lady Thornhill He got what he deserved.

Bridget (*off, calls*) Mr Hogarth? Are you here? Hallo!

Bridget enters, by the jetty. She wears a cloak. Lady Thornhill vanishes. William lies still.

(*Calls.*) Mr H? It's Bridget! Where are you?

She searches. William moans and stirs. Bridget sees him.

Mother of God!

Bridget helps William to sit up. He's groggy.

Are you hurt?

William Bridget –

Bridget (*calls*) Samuel!

William It was her.

Bridget What happened?

William My mother-in-law! She killed my dog!

Bridget Sir?

William Lady Thornhill! She poisoned Trump!

Bridget I don't think she did, sir.

William Yes, it was her, she admitted it, just now!

179

Bridget What do you mean, just now?

William When I was talking to her!

Bridget Here?

William Yes.

Bridget You can't have been.

William Why not?

Bridget Because –

William Are you saying I'm lying?

Bridget Sir, Lady Thornhill is dead. She passed away some hours ago. We've come to take you home.

William What do you mean, dead?

Bridget God love her, she's gone.

William But we was just talking! She spat at me, it's definitely her!

Bridget Whoever spat, it wasn't My Lady. She's dead.

William (*confused*) What are you talking about?

Bridget (*calls*) Sam! I've found him! Where are you, Sam? (*To William.*) Can you walk?

William Me legs is like jelly.

Bridget Sit here. We'll wait for Samuel.

William I'm cold.

Bridget wraps William in her cloak. They sit together.

Bridget There, I'm with you. Don't fret.

William What's happening, Bridget? What's going on?

Bridget thinks.

Bridget I don't know, sir. Seems to me that everything that happens is pure chance. It never crossed me mind I'd go to London. It never crossed me mind I'd end up with the nicest people anyone ever met. I have to conclude that it's an accident. Everything in life is an accident. God looks the other way, and things happen. That's the best explanation I can give.

William Bridget, I don't know what you're fucking talking about.

Bridget Ah, you've the bump on the head, you'll be grand.

Samuel enters by the jetty.

Samuel Where are you? Bridget!

Bridget Over here! He's been battered, so.

Samuel Right, Mr H, let's get you into the carriage.

William How'd you find me?

Samuel We asked at Strawberry Hill – they said you'd headed for the river.

William What's going on, Sam?

Samuel Lady Thornhill took poorly in town. There's nothing you can do, sir. She's had it.

They exit, helping William.

SCENE SIX

The Hogarths' garden in Chiswick. Dusk. Long shadows from the mulberry tree. On the bench lies Lady Thornhill's parasol. Jane enters with Mrs Colquhoun.

Jane Please, this way, Mrs Colquhoun.

Mrs Colquhoun I should like it if you would call me Hester.

Jane I am a little bit surprised, that you have –

Mrs Colquhoun I had to come. My behaviour this afternoon was reproachful. Mrs Ryott and I were in high spirits; it may be we had had too much cocoa; but to scorn and deride as we did? Well – it was disgusting behaviour, and I am ashamed.

Jane You have driven out here – to apologise?

Mrs Colquhoun Yes.

Jane No one's done anything as nice as that for as long as I can remember.

Mrs Colquhoun I should not have laughed. I'm so sorry.

Jane bursts into tears.

Oh, my dear Mrs Hogarth! What is it?

Mrs Colquhoun comforts Jane.

Jane My mother died.

Mrs Colquhoun Good gracious! When?

Jane This afternoon.

Mrs Colquhoun But she was – in Piccadilly she was –

Jane As unpleasant as ever, yes – but then she took a seizure – and she died!

Mrs Colquhoun Oh, you poor lamb! Here, sit down.

Jane sits on the bench. She finds the parasol. It upsets her.

Jane It's Mama's.

Mrs Colquhoun You have had a shock. Shall I fetch someone?

Jane No, I will be fine. Honestly. Just give me a moment. (*Pause.*) I tried to be a dutiful daughter. But I seemed to get everything wrong. I married for love; I know what she thought of that. Love! Thirty years of manoeuvring. And how many minutes of love? A child might have made all the difference. But that won't happen now. So what is left? What's left?

Mrs Colquhoun Friendship. Please let me be your friend. Now, is someone sitting with your mother?

Jane The Parson's here. He's laying her out in the painting room.

Mrs Colquhoun And Mr Hogarth?

Jane He'll be back soon, I hope.

Parson Venables enters from the painting room: an enthusiastic priest in a wide-brimmed hat.

Parson Venables All done, Mrs Hogarth.

Jane Parson Venables. This is Mrs Colquhoun.

Parson Venables Not *the* Mrs Colquhoun? An unalloyed pleasure.

Mrs Colquhoun May I ask – why have you laid out Lady Thornhill in the painting room?

Parson Venables It's cool, in there, with the curtains drawn. It has been a hot day today, which can be testing for a deceased person, as you know. (*To Jane.*) But she is with the angels now, in heaven.

Jane As long as it's not Chiswick, she'll be happy.

Parson Venables Your mother was devout, Mrs Hogarth. You must entertain no misgivings. She will enter the kingdom of heaven, and live in eternal bliss.

Mrs Colquhoun (*gently*) Let's hope there's plenty of cake.

Jane (*smiles*) Yes.

Jane and Mrs Colquhoun smile at each other. Samuel enters.

Samuel We've found him, ma'am.

Jane Oh, thank goodness.

William enters from the road, assisted by Bridget. He is muddied and bloodied, wigless, shoeless, coatless, with Bridget's cloak draped over his shoulders.
Jane, Mrs Colquhoun and Parson Venables are shocked at the sight.
William puts a brave face on it:

William Hello, dear. Pleasant day?

Jane Where have you been? Why are you bleeding? Where is your coat? Where are your shoes?

William I have a rather bad headache, do you mind if I –

He moves towards the house. Jane heads him off.

Jane Yes I do! Where have you been?

William considers his answer.

William I was down by the river at Twickenham, and –

Jane What were you doing down by the river at Twickenham?

William I was . . . fishing. Thought I'd try my hand at fishing. It's what blokes do when they retire. Who's she?

Jane This is my friend, Hester.

William Since when have you had a friend? I need to talk to you about your mother.

Jane William, my mother is –

William Your mother's out of order, that's what your mother is.

Mrs Colquhoun (*shocked*) Oh!

Jane Will, Mama is gone.

William Gone where?

Jane She's dead.

William Are you sure about that?

Jane (*to Samuel*) You told him?

Samuel Yes, of course.

Jane (*to William, angrily*) Why you are behaving like this? It's unforgivable. What have you been doing since I left you this morning?

William As I said, I decided, on a whim, to go angling, down Twickenham, in the hope of a perch, or a chub, when suddenly I was set upon by pirates –

Jane Pirates!

Parson Venables (*aside to Mrs Colquhoun*) A godless purlieu, Twickenham.

William Yeah, pirates, buccaneers, they come roiling up the river and they come ashore and –

Jane Twickenham does not have pirates! And you've never been fishing in your life! You're drunk!

William Drunk? I'm not drunk. I got whacked on the head, as it happens, by robbers who nicked my clothes, and I'm still not feeling right, and I might have dared to hope, Jane, for an ounce of human sympathy when at last I made it home.

Jane You'll get sympathy when you start telling the truth. Dear God!

William I think I better have a lie-down.

Abruptly, he turns and heads for the painting room.

Jane Don't go in there.

William It's my painting room, isn't it?

Jane Yes, but –

William So I'll go in it if I want. All right?

They all watch as William exits to the painting room.

Bridget (*aside to the Parson*) Is that where –?

Parson Venables nods.
They wait.
William re-enters from the painting room at speed.

William She's – she's –

Jane Yes, I was trying to tell you.

William Whose fucking idea was it to put that in my fucking studio? (*To Parson Venables.*) Yours?

Jane It was mine.

William takes Jane aside.

William Jane, the thing is, she isn't a hundred-per-cent dead. She spat on me, down by the river.

Jane Why would anyone say such a thing?

William And then I come home and she farts at me!

Jane What?

William Just then, when I went in. She saw it was me, so she let one off! Cor, the stink!

Parson Venables (*aside to Mrs Colquhoun*) That can happen.

Jane Bridget, your master is in a state of shock. The blow to the head has loosened his mind. Take him indoors, and give him a wash, and tend to his wounds, would you, please?

Bridget Ma'am. Come with me, sir.

Bridget steers William towards the house. They exit.

Jane Samuel, please stable the horses.

Samuel nods and exits to the road.

Parson, I should be most grateful if you would sit with Mother for a while.

Parson Venables I shall pray for her soul, ma'am.

He exits to the painting room.

Jane I think William's been with a woman.

Mrs Colquhoun What makes you say that?

Jane He has the stink of harlotry about him.

Mrs Colquhoun Why do you stand for it?

Jane I don't know. I am not his muse, I never was. We are not intimate. But when we were first married – when he was a nobody, with nothing to his name – he was, how to put it? Desirable.

Mrs Colquhoun I think he is a beast, my dear. I'm sorry.

Jane Well, we each have our cross to bear, Hester.

Mrs Colquhoun No, Jane, no. Self-sacrifice is not obligatory, not in any marriage. Were it myself exposed to public ridicule, I would think very hard about my future with the person responsible. And now, I am sure you will value some privacy, at this difficult time. I will go.

Jane Let me walk you to your carriage.

Mrs Colquhoun I do hope you will come to an assembly. You would fit in tremendously well.

Jane I should like that. Very much.

> *Jane and Mrs Colquhoun exit to the house.*
>   *Samuel enters and crosses the garden. Parson*
> *Venables comes out from the painting room, gasping.*

Samuel You surviving, Parson?

Parson Venables Some fresh air, and I shall rejoice.

Samuel Bit ripe in there, is it, sir?

Parson Venables These people are very unusual.

Samuel Yes, I know.

Parson Venables Have you been with them for long?

Samuel Since I was twelve. I lost my parents. They took me in.

> *Jane enters from the house. Parson Venables sees her*
> *and ducks back inside the painting room. It is starting*
> *to get dark.*

May I fetch you something, ma'am? Is there anything you'd like?

Jane I'd like my mama back, Sam. I'd like her to be sitting here, complaining.

Samuel My condolences.

Samuel turns to go, then turns back.

You done so much for us, Mrs Hogarth. Treated us as if we was your own family. Taught us all to read and write. You can count on me for anything, ma'am.

The sound of a horse riding up, fast. It comes to a clattering halt. Samuel is concerned. Then David Garrick enters at a run.

David Jane!

Jane Davy!

David I was visiting friends when news arrived that Will was attacked by the river. I left at once! Rode like the wind! I stand at my comrade's side.

Jane Oh, the sound of your voice.

David It is rather resonant this evening. Humidity, perhaps?

Jane (*to Samuel*) Go and get some supper. Thank you.

Samuel exits to the house.

David How is William?

Jane He's been drinking.

David Oh, no!

Jane I let him out of my sight for five minutes, and he comes home smelling like a brewery.

David God's hooks! He was fine when we parted.

Jane What were you doing? He tells me nothing but lies.

David We went for a walk.

Jane Where to?

David Strawberry Hill.

Jane Why did you go to Strawberry Hill?

David I didn't go to Strawberry Hill.

Jane You just said you did.

David No. Will did. I went home.

Jane What did he do there?

David I've no idea.

Jane Why did he suddenly decide to drink himself insensible? He's been sober for years!

David How I wish I could give you some answers. Is he badly hurt?

Jane He'll live. But my mother, I have to tell you, Davy, died this afternoon.

David Lady Thornhill? Did you say *died*?

Jane Yes, she's gone.

David Gone? But we were talking, here, by the mulberry tree!

Jane She took a fit, in Jermyn Street. We brought her home – alas – too late. She died.

David Oh, my poor Jane. 'Woe, destruction, ruin, and decay; The worst is death, and death will have his day.' Tell me how you feel.

Jane I feel empty.

David Empty? Like a shell? A pod? An integument?

Jane I cannot see the purpose of anything at all.

David Thank you for that. Useful. May I see her?

Jane Oh, David, would you? She loved your smile, you know.

David I know. I might give her a bit from *Julius Caesar*. What do you think? Appropriate?

Jane (*smiles*) She's laid out in the painting room. Shall I come too?

David No, don't. This task I face alone. Fie upon death! Fie upon't!

Jane Send out the Parson, would you?

David exits to the painting room. Jane watches him go with fondness. Parson Venables enters.

Parson Venables You wish to see me, ma'am?

Jane Allow Mr Garrick some time with my mother.

Parson Venables It *was* Mr Garrick! I thought so.

Jane Please do not get the idea, Mr Venables, that my husband is as bad-mannered as he appeared to be earlier. He has had some difficulties of late, and I think he is spiritually lost. He takes no pleasure in anything. He believes the world's against him. And the worst is – he despises me. Yet I do everything he asks.

Parson Venables You are his wife, pledged to honour and obey.

Jane Yes but, Parson, I'm not a drudge!

Parson Venables Madam. Your husband is an eminent man. He holds a royal appointment, and he is valued for his works of Christian charity. His endowment of the Foundling Hospital, that was a wonderful thing. Think of all the wretched orphans, who through him have come closer to God.

Jane But he's behaving like a madman! Like he's just got out of Bedlam!

Parson Venables The Almighty has seen fit to grant him genius. Who are we to understand the workings of his mind?

David enters from the painting room. He looks troubled.

Mr Garrick. Such a pleasure! I saw you in –

Jane I would rather Mother wasn't left alone.

Parson Venables Ah, yes, of course, the vigil.

He exits to the painting room.

David Jane, I am vexed.

Jane Why, what has happened, my dear?

David Nothing has happened. Except I have been lying. I lie and I lie, it's an instinct. But I can dissemble no longer. I realised, in there, that one day I may be called to account. And so: (*Beat.*) I saw the painting. 'Sigismunda'. I saw it yesterday. At the Exhibition. (*Gently.*) It's you.

Jane Yes.

David You are the Princess Sigismunda.

Jane It's me.

David Oh, Jane.

Jane I sat for it. I wish I hadn't.

David I know what you mean. I abhor being painted.

Jane I tried to resist. I've resisted for years. I let him do me once before; and it was absolutely awful. But I was persuaded that I had the face, the face he had to have. I was Sigismunda, weeping for Guiscardo. But really I was weeping for my life.

David Oh, by Jupiter! What has he done?

William, washed and dressed, enters from the house.

William What the fuck do you want?

Jane Oh, you are so rude!

She exits quickly to the house. William and David eye each other.

David I heard you took a beating.

William Where'd you hear that? Whilst you were posing for Joshua Reynolds?

David Now, Will –

William Done you with a couple of tarts, I gather?

David Let me explain –

William That's a knife in the guts, that is. That is a palpable hit. Why the fuck are you sitting to Joshua Reynolds?

David Will, please, consider how things stand. My profession is rarely given rank. We are but rogues and vagabonds, strolling players in a barn. If the finest portraitist in England wishes to paint me, who am I to object? I thereby strike a blow for Thespis! I thereby avow, that I am the equal of any of them – merchants, admirals, dukes! – and I dare to not be humble! Paint me! Put me in an eight-foot frame, that I may be adored! I deserve to be immortalised, for I have left my blood upon the boards of Drury Lane! (*Pause.*) Sometimes I actually listen to myself. It's alarming, isn't it? We are all of us foolish, Will. Foolish, vexatious, blind to our faults. But our friends must forgive us. Or what is the purpose of friends? (*Pause.*) I took your advice. I ordered a dog.

William A dog? What kind of a dog?

David A big one. A mastiff. A man's dog.

William What you going to call him?

David Dragon, I think.

William Jesus Christ.

David Will you throw a stick for Dragon? Can we still be friends?

William Why didn't you tell me you visit Horace Walpole?

David I don't visit Horace Walpole.

William Yes you do. Sunday lunch!

David That's lunch, that's hardly a *visit*!

William Next time I'll paint you as Judas.

David You judge me harshly. Nothing's ever black and white, Will. Oh, your engravings, your modern moral subjects, yes, but life, the lived life? It's muddy. It's a mess. It's all context. Why, not even Shakespeare dealt in moral absolutes. Shakespeare!

William is silent. David indicates the painting room.

I've been sitting in there talking to a corpse. Eventually, time runs out. Eventually, it's too late.

William is silent.

Why do you think I have so many friends? Because I'm ready to overlook their defects. And they're ready to overlook mine.

William is silent.

How many friends have you got, Will?

William is silent. David gives up.

Give my love to Jane.

David exits to his horse. We hear him riding away.
Parson Venables emerges from the painting room.

Parson Venables Is this a good moment?

William Perfect.

Parson Venables My name is Jasper Venables. I grew up in a house with your prints on the walls. 'Industry and Idleness'. 'Marriage à la Mode'. They inspired me to the sacraments of priesthood.

William What do you want?

Parson Venables I see before me a soul in torment. I see a life of sin, of venery, of despair.

William Have you been talking to my wife?

Parson Venables She has your best interests at heart, sir. She would have you turn aside from sin, and strive for the kingdom of heaven.

William But I like sin.

Parson Venables Pardon?

William I like it. I feed on it.

Parson Venables Sin?

William It's my favourite thing in the world.

Parson Venables I regret, I do not understand.

William No, well, you wouldn't, would you? You have given my wife some comfort, and that I thank you for. But now please take your cant and superstition and your rituals and relics and fuck off, all right, Reverend? Fuck off home.

Jane enters and listens, unseen. It's nearly dark.

Parson Venables I know you to be a moral man, sir, I know you are good at heart.

William How do you know that?

Parson Venables From your pictures.

William No, mate, I'm a sinner. I'm not a good man.

Parson Venables Are we being deliberately provocative? The Bishop has warned me of that.

William Shall I tell you how I come by this gash on me head? I picked up a prostitute down by the river. Round about your age, or younger. Poor and stupid. The taste of shame, like a mouthful of tar. But still I intended to fuck her. I was just about to do so when –

Jane That's enough! We do not want to hear it. Parson, you should go. Go home! Thank you.

Parson Venables The blessings of God be upon you both.

He exits. Jane and William circle each other.

Jane Have you no care for your immortal soul?

William You're joking.

Jane What were you doing at Strawberry Hill?

William Who says I was at Strawberry Hill?

Jane gives him a stern look.

Jane William.

William Mr Walpole and I had a schooner of sherry, and exchanged some remarks about dogs.

Jane Dogs?

William Yes.

Jane You didn't pick a fight?

William No, we was perfectly civil. Two men of the world. Then I saw your mother by the river.

Jane You did not see my mother by the river.

William She was very unkind about some parts of my anatomy.

Jane No, Will, she wasn't! She's dead!

William Matter of opinion. I saw her.

Jane Was this before or after you attempted to fornicate with a prostitute?

William is silent.

Because you swore you would stop all that.

William I didn't go looking for it, it just come along.

Jane The way you think about women is revolting.

William That is bumfluff, Jane. I love women. You're my princess, I worship at your feet.

Jane I don't want to be worshipped, you idiot! Don't put me on a pedestal – just talk to me once in a while!

William Look, Janey, I am an idiot, I know, and I make mistakes, I do – I'm flawed – but I love you, Jane. I love you. You're my wife.

Jane In town today I was ashamed of that.

William Ashamed of what?

Jane Being your wife.

William Why?

Jane Because the world has heard you painted me, and made poor work of it, too. I know I am plain, but is this what I deserve? To be derided as the ghastly Sigismunda? To be laughed at in public? In a tea-shop? (*Pause.*) I feel invaded, William, it's as if you have marched into me and staked out your territory, claimed me for the empire of art.

Can I tell you something? I hate art. I hate it. I hate painting, and drawing, and etching, and printing, all of it, it's useless. It just makes us unhappy, lonely and unhappy. I wish that it didn't exist! (*Pause.*) I'm going to go away.

William What?

Jane You can't treat me like this. I've had enough. I shall leave you and live by myself.

William What are you going to do all by yourself?

Jane (*shrugs*) Travel?

William (*appalled*) What, abroad?

Jane I hear Rome is remarkable.

William Fucking hell, Jane, what can they possibly have in Rome that we haven't got here? Look at it – the country cottage! The mulberry tree! The beautiful walled garden!

Jane Yes, I look at it, and I see my prison walls! I want to live differently. I want to have friends, I want to go out and do things, read, debate, explore – the world is full of wonder! I can't decay in Chiswick whilst others live lives of real achievement. I will go straight after the funeral.

William But – but – who am I going to talk to?

Jane (*bitterly*) Get another dog.

William You're not serious?

Lady Thornhill enters from the painting room. She wears her funerary shroud, her hair is down, and she clasps a Bible.

Lady Thornhill Of course she is, you bumptious oaf.

William spins and sees her. She is invisible to Jane.

William What?

Lady Thornhill What person of taste would entertain living with you?

William clutches at his head.

William Aah! Jane, I – Jane, I can see her!

Jane I beg your pardon?

William She's back! She's got out of her coffin!

Jane William, what's the matter?

William Can't you see her? Look!

Lady Thornhill I have not come for Jane.

Jane See who? What are you raving about?

William Your mother!

Jane My mother?

William Look, she's in her undies, look!

Jane Are you trying to offend me *again*?

William No, no!

Jane Because you're going the right way about it!

William Jane, I swear it, I can see her, she's just over there!

Jane Oh, for pity's sake. Strange, isn't it, that these things never happen when you're sober?

William Please!

Lady Thornhill This is almost as good as Drury Lane.

Jane Don't come near me tonight. Don't come in the house. Stay away.

William But where will I sleep?

Jane I don't care!

Jane goes into the house. We hear the door shut and bolted. It's now quite dark.

William Jane!

Lady Thornhill beckons William towards the painting room.

Lady Thornhill Are you coming? Are you ready? Come to bed.

William No, I'm not ready! I've got things to do!

Lady Thornhill So much to accomplish. So little time.

William Fuck off back to hell, you dead bitch!

Lady Thornhill La! – The language.

In good humour, Lady Thornhill exits to the painting room.

William Jane! Let me in! She's after me! Janey! Am I losing my wits?

No response.

My head is full of pictures, and they won't go away. I didn't mean to offend you – I was just doing my work! Just trying to stay in the game! But nothing is worth nothing if I'm not with my wife. I love you, darling. I do. My head hurts. Open the door.

No response.

All right, then. It will stop. I will never paint again. I will never hold a palette. I will never shape a brush. My last and final painting is the Princess Sigismunda. That is a solemn promise.

No response.

Christ, open the door, you stupid woman! My head hurts!

He sinks to his knees.

I'm tired, I'm so tired. The battle's over, the bastards won. I feel dizzy, like – falling from the sky – like – terrifying – Jane! I've got this fucking banging in my skull!

Lady Thornhill (*off*) William? Come to bed!

William No!

He suffers a seizure – perhaps a stroke. He sinks to the ground, unable to speak. Lady Thornhill vanishes. The house door is unbolted and Bridget runs out.

Bridget Sir! Mr Hogarth! What's happened?

She helps William into the house.

SCENE SEVEN

One year later, in the garden at Chiswick. The sun shines and the birds sing. Samuel is fixing bunting around the garden: there's going to be a party. Bridget enters with the coffee things. She lays them out on the table.

Samuel Don't forget the cream.

Bridget I'll not. I'm that excited!

Samuel You just mind the master, Bridget. Make sure he doesn't get frightened.

Bridget How many carriages is coming?

Samuel Four.

He exits to the house. William enters from the painting room. He looks much older, and not very well. He walks with a stick.

Bridget Good morning, sir. Your coffee's there.

It becomes apparent that William can no longer speak properly. He tries to get the words out, but only produces approximate sounds.

William Fah ooo, Berjj.

He eases himself on to the bench and drinks his coffee.

Bridget The big day today, and a grand day for it, too.

William Orff – orff –

Bridget Yes, the orphans. And the mistress is just arrived from town! 'Tis a pleasure to see her, looking so bright and so happy.

William Ih she?

Bridget Well, sir, she's out of mourning now. She's laughing, and as pretty as a picture! Oh, here they come.

Jane enters from the house with Mrs Ryott and Mrs Colquhoun. They wear bright, gay dresses. They're cheerful. Though it's hard for him, William rises politely.

Jane Good morning, William. How are you feeling today?

William Aw rye fahh oo.

Jane You remember Mrs Colquhoun? And Mrs Ryott?

William attempts to bow to the ladies. Bridget bobs and exits.

Mrs Ryott Your garden is charming, Mr Hogarth. I expect you enjoy the pretty flowers?

Jane He potters about, don't you, dear? Sit down, now.

William sits.

Mrs Ryott He seems in fair spirits.

Jane He can do very little for himself. But he causes no trouble. – I have to tell you, William, that I am shutting up the house in Leicester Fields. My friends and I tire of London. We are planning a long trip.

Mrs Ryott We are venturing to Switzerland! Is that not audacious?

William Witza?

Mrs Colquhoun Yes, Mont Blanc, Chamonix, the famous Sea of Ice!

Mrs Ryott We are converts to the picturesque, you see. The violence of the mountains, the turmoil of the lakes.

William Doh ike. Ike Issick.

Jane I know you like Chiswick. That's why I'm leaving you here. Bridget and Samuel will see to you. We shall be abroad for several months.

William Wih oo rye?

Jane Of course. – Now, the children are coming today, you are aware of this?

William nods.

Mrs Colquhoun Which children are these, Jane?

Jane From the Foundling Hospital. William used to be on the Board. Once a year, when the fruit is ripe, we bring them here to feast themselves on mulberries and cream. They very much enjoy it.

Mrs Colquhoun Well, that is a splendid tradition.

Jane We think it the least we can do, don't we, dear? Now, William, the ladies and I are going for a walk. If the foundlings arrive before we return – sit quietly, understand? They will not harm you.

William Oo gg win far?

Jane No, just a turn round Chiswick Park.

Mrs Ryott We must get fit to scale those Alps! Good day, Mr Hogarth.

William rises stiffly.

William Goo ay, ay dees.

Mrs Colquhoun Good day to you, sir.

William (*to Jane*) Enjoy orss eff.

Jane kisses William on the cheek.

Jane I love you.

The ladies exit. William eases himself back on to the bench. Samuel enters from the stables.

Samuel We're going to be invaded, guv. There's about thirty children.

William Fuh gg ell.

Samuel grins and exits to the house. William takes from his pocket a scrap of paper and a pencil. He jots down notes. He thinks, chews the end of his pencil, drinks his coffee.
Lady Thornhill enters from the painting room. She is beautifully dressed, with her parasol. William rises from his seat. Suddenly he can speak and move normally.

Good morning.

Lady Thornhill Good morning.

William How are you today, My Lady?

Lady Thornhill Tip-top.

Lady Thornhill sits, then William sits next to her.

What are you writing?

William Some notes for my new book.

Lady Thornhill Have you a title?

William *An Apology for Painters.*

Lady Thornhill Your best yet. If you run out of things to apologise for, you know who to ask.

William (*smiles*) I do.

Lady Thornhill fans herself.

Lady Thornhill It is devilish hot.

William I wonder why.

Lady Thornhill I wouldn't look too smug, if I were you.

William Fair enough. But was it worth it, do you think?

Lady Thornhill Was what worth what?

William It seems only yesterday I was shimmying up the greasy pole, hand over hand, fighting to get to the top. Then you wake up one morning and it's over. And you think, what was that all about?

Lady Thornhill Did you get to the top?

William It's a fiddle. There isn't a top.

Lady Thornhill Really? I heard there was.

In the distance, we hear the sounds of excited children disembarking from carriages.

William But the pain and the tears and the fisticuffs, for the sake of a few dozen paintings? I mean, really? I was all fire and indignation, I was burning up, and now? Can't even get a stiffy.

Lady Thornhill Oh, dear – is that all you can think about? (*Pause.*) I can hear an unconscionable racket.

William It's the orphans and foundlings, coming for their fruit.

Lady Thornhill Good grief.

William Jane loves to see the children.

Lady Thornhill So do you, I think.

William I'm fascinated by their faces. The innocence and the fear. All that is to come, and how soon it will be over. Life is a very strange thing.

Lady Thornhill Yes, but there's no need to encourage them.

William I disagree. We will give a little pleasure while we can.

Bridget enters with a jug of cream. She can't see Lady Thornhill.

Bridget Have you finished your coffee, sir?

William Ehh. Fah ooo.

Bridget Here's the cream for the kiddies.

Bridget puts down the cream. William dips his finger in.

William Veh ice.

Bridget Hands off!

She clears away the coffee things, and exits. Lady Thornhill dips her finger in the cream, and licks it.

Lady Thornhill Cream. How lovely. I have a message from your dog.

William Did you say you have a message from my dog?

Lady Thornhill Yes.

William What, from Trump?

Lady Thornhill Why, oh, why did you give him such a ridiculous name? Trump? In all honesty? Trump? Could you not have called the creature something sensible? Like Rex, for example? Or Blinky?

William (*laughing*) Blinky?

Lady Thornhill What is so amusing? I had a Blinky once.

William Did you?

Lady Thornhill Yes.

William Blinked a lot, did he?

Lady Thornhill Oddly enough, he did. The absurdly named Trump has asked me to pass on a message. He would like you to know that he is well, and cared for, and he looks forward to seeing you soon.

William Trump said that?

Lady Thornhill Yes.

William . . . Right.

> *William, very surprised and moved, digests this news. The sounds of the children get louder.*

Lady Thornhill (*groans*) They will be upon us in a minute. Then they will gorge themselves and vomit. Little beasts.

William My dad would have loved it – coming out from Smithfield to a place like this. He would have stuffed his face and been sick in the flowerbed.

Lady Thornhill I take it he didn't amount to much?

William No. He didn't. He listened to great men's promises, silly sod. That's why I struck out for meself. (*Pause.*) Good luck, Dad.

The children are approaching, laughing and shrieking and calling to each other.

Lady Thornhill Well, we should go soon. Are you ready?

William Not quite. I have to finish an engraving.

Lady Thornhill I thought you had given up art? Or did art give up you? I forget.

William I said I'd quit painting. I never mentioned prints.

Lady Thornhill The subject of this marvellous gravure?

William The end of everything. The death of Time.

Lady Thornhill Oh, delicious.

William I thought I'd do a limited edition. Two shillings and sixpence. What do you think?

Lady Thornhill Cheap at the price.

William Exactly.

The children get nearer and nearer, until we are awash in their excited voices. William and Lady Thornhill sit peacefully and listen. William smiles.

The End.